Ordinary

ANGELS

Ordinary
ANGELS

SHARON STEVENS EVANS

ENCOURAGE
PUBLISHING
NEW ALBANY, INDIANA

Printed in the United States of America

For worldwide distribution

Library of Congress Control Number 2023942401

Cataloging data:
Evans, Sharon Stevens
Ordinary Angels

1. Autobiography and biography/personal memoir 2. Autobiography and biography/religious 3. Religion/Christian Living/Inspirational 4. Religion/ Christian Living/Personal growth 5. Religion/Christian Living/Afterlife 6. Religion/Christian Living/Calling & Vocation

Dewey Decimal Classification: 818.5, 248.843

Edited by Leslie Turner

Cover and interior design by Jonathan Lewis

Back cover photograph by Bruce Morris

Scripture quotations are taken from the New American Standard Bible® 1995 (NASB1995), Copyright © 1960, 1971, 1977, 1995 by The Lockman Foundation. All rights reserved.

ISBN 978-1-960166-12-8 (paperback, ebook)
ISBN 978-1-960166-15-9 (hardcover)
ISBN 978-1-960166-13-5 (audiobook)

Published by:
Encourage Publishing, New Albany, Indiana
www.encouragepublishing.com

A note about privacy

MANY OF THE names in this story have been changed to protect the privacy of their family members. There are also many who contributed to this story or whose names have always been part of the public history, and the author extends her deep appreciation and acknowledgment for everyone's role in this amazing story. We have done our best to confirm facts, time line, and details in Sharon's story, though certainly those who were there have different perspectives and memories. We are glad to be able to bring Sharon's recollections to you as well as accounts from many others close to the story and know you will be blessed.

Contents

Prologue

SHARON STEVENS, twice divorced, barely making enough to support herself, would never claim to be an angel. In fact, her life was full of chaos and risk from the moment she was born.

Early in life, perilous situations were thrust upon her. As an adult, she gravitated toward adventure and spur-of-the-moment decisions that often put her on the precipice of disaster and kept her in the pathway of people who would take advantage of her. If your aim is to find fault with her, she would be an easy target, but look again.

This diminutive hair stylist was not the person you would have chosen for such a monumental task with a life hanging in the balance—but God chose her, nonetheless. And where you or I would probably have done whatever was the very least we could do, Sharon said yes to the impossible.

She might never have risked everything she had to help a complete stranger but for the events that unfolded that unusually cool Kentucky August morning.

1

The Article

A t some time or another, we all wonder what our destiny in life will be. Will our legacy be something we carefully strive to make happen, or does God have a mysterious plan for us to figure out—something we are supposed to say yes to? We wonder, when we die, what will we be most remembered for?

When that day came for me, the day I figured out what I was supposed to say yes to, I could never have imagined all the ways I had been preparing for this assignment all of my life. Every person who hurt me, every person who helped me in some way, who stepped in as my very own angel, had a part in it. God didn't waste any of it. Not a single tear.

And through all those things I experienced during my life—both acts of violence and of kindness—through God's constant protection over me, I had my moment to become an angel to someone else. And in turn, that sweet child became an angel to me and so many others.

I had no idea that beautiful summer morning in August of 1992, as I woke up and got ready to start my fast-paced day as a hairstylist, that my "calling" was about to tap me on the shoulder.

As I sat down at my kitchen table drinking my first cup of coffee, I read through the *Courier-Journal*'s morning edition. It was then that I came upon the most heartbreaking article I had ever read.

"LOUISVILLE FAMILY IS BEARING UP UNDER CRUSHING BURDEN OF CRISES," the story title read. My eyes were drawn to the adorable faces of two small girls sitting on the lap of a beautiful young woman. Jim Adams, the columnist, often wrote human interest stories about people or events in the community, but this story was different. There was an urgency about it. I started to read:

> *Basically, Ed Schmitt looked OK, considering. Yes, there were dark circles under the eyes, several days' growth of beard, a weariness in his shoulders, hair rebelling. But his constitution was firm, and just about everyone who knows him says the same thing: I don't see how he holds up so well.*

> *The concept of a health-care crisis isn't news to the Schmitt family of 243 Alpha Avenue in Buechel. Crisis has made itself a member of the family.*

> *Daughter Ashley, age 4, received a new liver last year at the University of Nebraska Medical Center in Omaha, and her only sibling, fragile Michelle, 20 months and 16 pounds, is in need of a liver transplant, too. Both have biliary atresia.*[1]

I had never heard of biliary atresia, but I knew that a liver transplant was a difficult surgery for anyone, much less a sick little child. I knew that finding a match could take some time. I folded the newspaper to frame the article and kept reading.

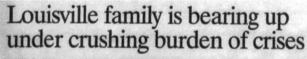

Louisville family is bearing up under crushing burden of crises

Basically, Ed Schmitt looked OK, considering. Yes, there were dark circles under the eyes, several days' growth of beard, a weariness in his shoulders, hair rebelling. But his constitution was firm, and just about everyone who knows him says the same thing: I don't see how he holds up so well.

JIM ADAMS
METRO COLUMNIST

and Theresa have been worn into the ground — he at the auto-parts shop where he works, she at home with the children, where she's been full time since last year, when she left her job with the Jefferson County clerk.

"Since Ashley was born, I've worked 70, 80 hours a week, and

Yet, the most pressing Schmitt crisis today has to do with neither Ashley nor Michelle. This time it's their mother, Ed's wife: Theresa A. Schmitt, 29, has been in the intensive care unit of Baptist Hospital East for more than a month. A machine is breathing for her, at what doctors call a high level of life support.

It started with difficulty breathing, progressed like lightning into an overwhelming pneumonia, then to Adult Respiratory Distress Syndrome. As a complication, doctors also suspect an uncommon vascular disorder called Wegener's granulomatosis.

It's no exaggeration to say her life has been seriously threatened.

So Ed Schmitt has been living with crisis.[3]

I looked at the photo again. Right at that moment, that beautiful young mother of two was fighting for her life in a hospital ICU unit with two critically ill children at home with her overwhelmed husband.

My heart was stirring as I clutched the paper, my coffee growing cold. I read slowly, stopping and staring out the window, deep in thought. In the next paragraph, the readers heard from the young father.

"Since Ashley was born, I've worked 70, 60 hours a week, and not done as much as I should have. But you've got to pay the bills, and you've got to buy their medicines."

The first week Theresa was here in the hospital, "she started going downhill. They made the decision to open her up and do a lung biopsy. She couldn't stand to be moved down to the operating room, so the next thing I knew half the operating room was coming down the hall here, and they operated on Theresa back in the ICU."[4]

To summarize how everything began for this sweet little family, by 1992, Ed and Theresa Schmitt had been married twelve years, and like most young couples, expected to live happily ever after. But for them, tragedy after tragedy cruelly surfaced, interrupting their dreams of happiness from the beginning.

From the outset, Ed and Theresa had planned to raise a family. They were both hardworking people, confronting the everyday tasks of building a home and future together. Theresa was a beautiful, intelligent, fun-loving, twenty-one-year-old when they married, respected at the county clerk's office. Ed had served his time in the army, and after his release, he went to work in corrections.

After four years, Theresa and Ed learned they were finally going to have a baby. The joy they felt was overwhelming as they prepared to welcome their little bundle of joy.

Theresa gave birth to a beautiful baby girl, whom they named Ashley. Like most young couples, they hoped for their child to be in good health. They were amazed at this tiny, little creature they had produced and proudly enjoyed all the special moments of their precious child's birth, their spirits high.

FAMILY PHOTO
In a recent family snapshot, Theresa A. Schmitt, 29, posed with her daughters Ashley, 4, and Michelle, 20 months old.

© The Courier-Journal – USA TODAY NETWORK
Photo courtesy of and by licensed with USA Today/Imagn

While in the hospital, Theresa began to notice that something wasn't quite right with her newborn daughter. The doctors alerted the parents that their baby had a severe medical condition. She was born with a deadly liver disorder called biliary atresia; she would require a liver transplant to survive.

Without a transplant, little Ashley would likely not live to her third birthday. From this day forward, their lives would never be the same, but Ed and Theresa would remain firm in their resolve to address the issues facing their tiny daughter.

I paused and set the paper down, a tear rolling down my cheek. For most of us, such childhood diseases are a rarity, but I couldn't help but think of the births of my own healthy boys and imagine how devastating it would be to learn that one of them suffered from a life-threatening disease. As parents, we want to protect our children from every danger, particularly when they are so young and vulnerable. The truth is, we can't. Ed and Theresa couldn't, and neither could you nor I.

I stared out the window as I thought about the Schmitts, and about my own journey as a single parent, remembering one particularly frightening incident my oldest son, Derek, experienced as a young child.

2

A New Gear

After my separation from Derek's father (a story you will learn more about later) I settled back in Louisville near my parents. Needing to support myself and my son, I decided to use my experience gained on the road with my husband's band, where I dressed hair for a number of well-known celebrities, including David Crosby, The Byrds, Paul Revere and the Raiders, and many more. As I started my career as a hair designer, my parents watched Derek during the day while I was at work. As with most boys, Derek was very rambunctious, even as a little two-year-old. So, to keep him from getting into too much mischief, I bought him a kitten—and they became the best of friends.

My father wouldn't allow the kitten in the house, so Derek played with him outside. One day I drove over to pick Derek up and saw Mom, Dad, and the neighbors frantically scouring the bushes around the house and the property next door.

I parked the car and strode up the walkway to the house. My father turned to me; the haunted look on his face said everything.

"What's going on, Dad?"

"Don't be alarmed, but Derek's gone missing."

"Missing? What do you mean by 'missing'?" Of course, I was immediately alarmed.

He explained that Derek had learned to unlock the back door. "Today when he woke up from his nap," my father explained, "he must have walked into the backyard."

My mind was racing. I asked, "How long has he been gone?"

"About an hour," he responded. "The police are on their way."

My heart sank and I began to tremble. Like every mother, I feared the worst, imagining him being kidnapped or wandering off into the street behind the house and getting run over.

Tears now pouring from my eyes as I struggled not to panic, I immediately joined the search, calling out and hoping that he was just hiding, and that hearing his mommy's voice would draw him out. One of his favorite games was hide-and-seek and, given his small size, Derek always hid *under* things.

I walked around to the backyard, stood there, and surveyed the lawn from the patio. That's when I spotted his inflatable swimming pool, which was flipped upside down. I saw some bouncing and bumping movement under it and felt instantly relieved.

I quietly approached the pool and gently raised it. Derek's big blue eyes looked up at me. I was so glad to find him that I didn't know whether to scold my little toddler or hug him. He and his tiny kitten had been under the pool for over an hour on a warm day. He could have suffocated easily in that time or suffered from heatstroke. Miraculously, both he and his sweet pet seemed unharmed. *When Derek heard all the thrashing about and heard his grandparents and neighbors calling out for him, he must have thought they were all* playing "hide and seek," I thought to myself. I picked Derek up and held him tight, walking to the front of the house, Derek with his kitten in his arms, just as the police cars arrived.

My eyes were swollen with tears as I handed Derek over to my mother's arms. I kept clutching the kitten as I explained where I found my son.

My father took the kitten from me and said to the little animal, "Okay, you can stay in the house."

Derek's eyes lit up, and he said, "Good, Papa, good."

• • •

As I THOUGHT back to that day so long before, I remembered other moments when my own son had been in circumstances far more dangerous than this. I stood up from the table and stepped over to the coffee maker to pour myself another cup. I looked out into the backyard and could almost see that yellow plastic pool.

For any parent, a situation like a lost child reminds us just how precious and fragile the lives of our children and loved ones are. But, of course, that brief moment in my memory could not compare to the fear and powerlessness this father felt, with the lives of both of his children, then his beloved wife, in jeopardy.

My thoughts returned to the Schmitt family's tragic situation, and I sat down to continue reading the article.

At some point during that week, one doctor "told me she probably wouldn't make it through the day."

Since then, his has been a daily vigil, along with various family members and a wide assortment of people touched by the family with triple crises. . . .

Many others—from the Southeast Area Ministries, to the Fern Creek Business and Community Association, to the Buechel-Fern Creek Jaycees—have asked what they can do to help.

Ed Schmitt simply wants to say thanks to everyone.

"What are the odds of me having two kids with the same disease, and have my wife go down with some disease? Odds of that are tremendous, so I don't believe in odds.

"It's day to day. If Theresa does come through this, she's talking about a long period of rehabilitation. I mean a super long time of rehabilitation. I haven't thought about it, to be honest. I just live day to day. I know that somewhere down the road, the load's got to get lighter."[5]

I had endured hardships both as a child and a parent myself. It was as if this little family's trials were awakening all of those emotions all over again, tugging at my heart, and reigniting the fears that used to haunt me. I questioned myself. I was in no position to help them, to make any real difference, was I? As I finished reading the article, a voice inside me grew stronger and stronger, telling me to help.

Less than twenty years earlier, I was a young mother whose life was in the hands of a team of doctors, my family told I would likely not survive—yet, I did. Everything I learned that day so long ago, as I lay hovering between life and death, was coming back to me now, filling me with peace and courage. I decided in that moment to listen, to say yes, and to act.

I had no idea what that commitment would mean, exactly what the needs were, how hard it would become, how long it would last, nor how many other people would become involved. I had no idea how deeply this decision would change my life.

My heart found a new gear that morning. The article called forth a remarkable sense of purpose inside of me as I focused on the duty to serve those sweet faces smiling at me from that newspaper article. I was quickly becoming more and more connected to this family and the terrible situation they faced. My alarm clock rang, set to alert me that I had thirty minutes to drive to the hair salon where I worked. *Perfect timing*, I thought. Learning about Michelle's diagnosis was too much for me to digest.

I folded the newspaper and put it in my purse, turned off the coffee maker, and headed out the door. It was a cool morning, and as I drove to work, I couldn't help but feel overwhelmed by the task ahead of me. Yet, I did not doubt that my life's mission was to help this family. I had no idea, as my mind began to brainstorm possible solutions, that my complicated past had uniquely prepared me for all that lay ahead.

Throughout the day as I worked styling clients' hair, I could not stop thinking about the Schmitt family. I wanted to learn everything I could. What had the last four years been like for this family? What did it mean to have biliary atresia, and how risky was it for the Schmitts to have Michelle after seeing their firstborn, Ashley, go through so much? In time, I would learn as much as I could about the condition, and about all the family was going through.

3

Ashley's Day

MARCH 1991

In 1991, biliary atresia affected roughly one out of every 15,000 births in the United States. Scientists still do not know the cause. The nature of this deadly disease would eventually trigger a series of painful side effects. Little Ashley's jaundiced skin constantly itched, causing her to scratch herself, even in her sleep, leaving scabs and open sores. In addition, her tiny enlarged liver put uncomfortable pressure on other organs, a condition that often leads to other organ malfunctions and severe damage. The only cure was a liver transplant, but even with a transplant, she would have a lifetime of issues to face.

Her body would not absorb food well, causing vitamin deficiencies and weakening her immune system. As a result, Ashley would become even more vulnerable and frail, falling victim to disease and viruses. The required medications were very harsh on her delicate tissues. As this disease progressed, spontaneous internal bleeding became a constant threat that could instantly kill the child.

The road ahead for the Schmitt family was going to be long and hard, but like any parents, Ed and Theresa were determined to pursue options that would heal their daughter, or at least improve her quality of life, even though they were not wealthy by any means.

Caring for Ashley was such a joy for this loving couple. Ed and his ailing daughter became great buddies, and Theresa enjoyed watching their gentle play on the blanket spread over the living room rug.

Theresa had always wanted multiple children, raised to be close and supportive of each other through the years. Theresa's parents had died when she was relatively young. She knew the loneliness of a solitary existence—until she met Ed.

While it would be difficult having another child to raise with Ashley needing so much extra care, Theresa felt that having a healthy sibling by her side might give Ashley the motivation to persist and get stronger. While they waited for news of a liver donor, the young couple had lots of questions for Ashley's specialist. Would another pregnancy be safe? Was Ashley suffering because of something in their genes that could be passed on to another child? He assured them that Ashley's condition was not hereditary, and highly unlikely to reoccur.

They were relieved to hear this news and made plans for a second child. Theresa soon found herself happily expecting another baby. She and Ed continued giving Ashley the consistent, special care she needed while Theresa's baby bump grew. The next few months flew by, and on December 3, 1990, Michelle Leigh Schmitt was born. Theresa's fears rose as she held Michelle for the first time, remembering Ashley's complications. None of baby Michelle's tests revealed any issues, but Theresa's feelings of uneasiness remained as she brought Michelle home, carefully examining her baby very closely day after day, looking for any signs of a problem.

Ashley was two and a half and while she doted over her beautiful newborn baby sister, the family nervously awaited the call that the doctors had a liver match for Ashley. Christmas came and went, and as the days ticked by, their daughter's condition worsened; Ed and Theresa feared it would soon be too late for little Ashley. Then, early in 1991, the call came.

While Theresa rapidly packed their bags, Ed became frantic, having second thoughts about such a delicate operation. Theresa stopped packing and went over to sit down beside him on the bed. "Let's talk about this," she said softly.

With tears running down his face, Ed's fears came tumbling out. "I can't let her go. She's so weak and sick. She may not survive the surgery. I just can't put her through it."

Theresa gently placed a hand on his face, pulling him near her. "I'm afraid too, but she's suffering, and it's only going to get worse.

This surgery is our one chance for her to have a long life, free of her constant pain."

"Theresa, I'm so scared of losing her!" he cried out.

"I know, but we must forget our fears and trust God to provide for her needs. We can't think of ourselves," she said, looking directly into Ed's eyes. "Let's give Ashley that one chance."

Theresa's plea reached the panic-stricken father, and they quickly finished preparing for the trip. By now, they only had six hours to cross the country from Louisville to the hospital in Omaha, Nebraska, for the harvested liver to be transplanted.

A charter flight was reserved and ready to take off but would not leave until the $5,200 payment was made. Ed's parents had agreed to use their savings to bankroll the flight, but there was a hold on the funds at the bank.

Time was running out. When the check finally cleared, they boarded their plane and were soon airborne and on their way to Omaha. An ambulance was waiting at the other end to quickly take Ashley to the hospital.

Ashley came through the nine-hour surgery successfully. She would have to live on costly medication for the rest of her life, but she was alive and would soon be a healthy, rosy-cheeked little girl.

During the first few weeks of Ashley's recuperation in Omaha, Theresa enjoyed caring for newborn Michelle at Ashley's bedside, now sure that the worst was over for Ashley.

After months in Omaha, Ed was glad to finally bring his family home again, relieved that the whole ordeal was over. Life seemed to be slowly but surely heading back in the right direction. The young couple had massive bills to contend with, but after watching their child's brush with death, they would find a way to work through it, and time was now on their side.

Ashley required intense home care at this stage. She would be attached to medical filtration tubes for some time. Restricting the movements of a three-year-old child who felt good for the first time in her life was quite a task for the young mother, but Theresa found a way, and had help from Ed's mother when she needed to rest.

Not long after Ashley's liver transplant, Theresa began to feel ill. She had a long-lasting cold she couldn't shake, but her doctor told her it was nothing serious. As days turned into weeks and Theresa immersed herself in the routine of caring for both her girls while Ed worked as many hours as he could to cover the bills, Theresa set aside concerns about herself as her keen motherly instincts continued to tell her "Something is not right with Michelle."

Weeks passed, and Theresa's own symptoms continued to hang on. By the time Michelle was three months old, Theresa's instincts about her infant would prove to be right. Michelle was not gaining weight, and other symptoms began to appear.

Against all odds, Michelle was also diagnosed with biliary atresia, the same life-threatening condition that afflicted Ashley. Once again, the defenseless young couple faced the long, dreadful threat of death now plaguing their second daughter. In the meantime, Theresa's own health continued to deteriorate.

4

Dark Secret

1946–1958

When you experience hardship from the beginning of life, you are too young to know the cruelty of your circumstances and too innocent to understand the injustice. This was so true for Ashley and Michelle, and perhaps was one reason why I was so drawn to them; in a very different way, I also experienced cruel and unjust circumstances as a child, with lifelong consequences. Unlike these tiny sisters, I had no one in my life to protect me. As I read about Ed and Theresa, I was so glad the girls had such loving parents to care for them, something I had longed for most of my life.

• • •

I WAS RAISED by a hardworking, middle-class couple. From the outside looking in, it seemed to everyone as if I was growing up in a nice family, in a comfortable home surrounded by a white picket fence in the suburbs of Louisville, Kentucky. It wasn't until I became old enough to recognize that my parents were severe alcoholics that I realized how alone I truly was. My experiences as a child created problems and left deep scars for many years, yet even the pain of that affliction taught me some important values.

When I was a toddler and my parents wanted to go drinking, they took me with them, frequently patronizing the local taverns on weekends, week after week, year after year, while they partied with their friends. Occasionally, other children who were in the

15

same situation would join me, and we would play together. Generally, my "bar mates" were older boys teaching me to throw rocks and spit in the parking lot, but it filled the lonely gaps of time. In this adult environment, I was so innocent and vulnerable; however, I soon gained a sense of when a threat was headed my way and quickly learned how to stay out of the path of dangerous people. I most certainly must have had someone watching over me during those early years, but even as a young child, I began building an invisible wall of protection, keeping to myself as much as possible.

I learned to put myself to bed in strange places when I was very young, even falling asleep in the wrong person's car in the parking lot one night. I learned to drive by the time I was twelve years old, often driving my parents home after a night of drinking. This made my father proud enough to brag, telling his friends how well he had trained me.

Witnessing my parents in these drunken states would later leave me feeling disgusted and abandoned, but I learned independence. I had to be strong enough to "parent" my parents, making responsible decisions for them while I was still a child. It taught me to be cautious and protective of the weaker ones around me, and it elevated my resolve to take life more seriously than my parents had.

On the other hand, my mother and father were very devoted to each other and were a very loving pair. I never witnessed them having a cross word with one another during my early life with them. My mother honored my father and lived her life solely for him, loving him as I have never seen any woman love a man.

I was not as fortunate to have that kind of close relationship with my mother. Her drinking eventually worsened, all but destroying any loving relationship between us. As the years went on, while my father put in a hard day's work, my mother would daily cover her kitchen table with empty beer bottles.

She was a dutiful mother in many respects, but in time the alcohol seemed to destroy her gentle mind, and she suffered severe mood swings. Looking back, I could see that perhaps the alcohol was masking a deeper mental health condition, but as a child, I simply learned how to read her condition. She had become unpredictable, was easily agitated, and the loneliness from having to avoid her at such times took its toll on me.

When I was about twelve years old, my concern for my parents became a major factor in my life. As I became more aware of the effects of alcohol on our lives, I grew embarrassed by their routine of drunkenness. I began to question my mother's heavy drinking.

I could see she was growing sicker; alcoholism was affecting her mind and her once practical way of doing things. When I spoke up, she refused to change and saw my disapproval as a threat. I learned quickly not to say anything more about her drinking, but I wanted so much to save my mother from her self-destruction. When sober, she was a sweet woman, but she was unable, and unwilling, to change on her own power.

It was during this period of my early teenage years when I lost touch with her as her daughter; she saw my longing to escape the alcoholic atmosphere our household imposed on me. It was a tough situation to be in as an only child. There were no sisters or brothers to vent my feelings to or share the closeness only siblings can understand.

As I began to make friends in junior high school, I was ashamed of my dysfunctional home life and tried to hide it. It was my deep, dark secret that I didn't want anybody else to know. This sense of shame hindered my social development and created problems that took years for me to understand and overcome.

I wanted to be respected and grow up like the other kids. I yearned to be proud of my family and my home, to someday adopt the good values of a healthy culture, but I had to seek those values outside of my home. I found myself visiting friends and watching how "normal" families interacted with each other.

5

Twenty-Nine

AUGUST 13, 1992

That night after a long day at the hair salon, I fixed myself dinner and cleaned up, sat down in the living room, and took out the morning paper from my purse. I started to re-read the Schmitt story.

The writer delved into the enormous expense of Ashley's transplant surgery. This debt would overwhelm any young family starting out, and they still needed to plan for Michelle's transplant. But how were they going to pay for it?

While these concerns were pressing them, Theresa's cold symptoms continued to worsen, and her lungs began to hurt. Caring for Ashley in her fragile condition plus an equally vulnerable newborn baby would have been a stressful situation for anybody. She wondered, was there more to her symptoms?

Theresa made several trips to her doctor and was repeatedly told her ailment was just a bad cold, her system weakened by exhaustion. She felt it was more severe and continually reached out for help, but no one took her seriously.

She wondered, *Who has a cold for over a year? What if it's something else? Am I exposing my sick children to a bacterial or viral infection?* If either one of her girls caught something from her, recovery could easily require a two-week hospital stay for them.

Within the year, Theresa's condition worsened, and she was finally admitted to the hospital. She was first diagnosed with pneumonia, but she did not respond to the antibiotic treatment. After further testing, she was diagnosed with a rare autoimmune disorder, granulomatosis, which at the time was known as Wegener's disease. Caught early, chances of recovery are good, but Theresa's diagnosis came over a year into her illness.

Theresa's condition quickly deteriorated, and she was put on a life-support system made up of tubes and machines. Hour by hour, she struggled to take her next breath, unable to see her children, hanging on to every precious moment. While Ed's mother, Barbara, cared for their two girls at home, the family waited. They waited for the phone call that a liver was available for tiny Michelle, and they waited to see if Theresa would beat the odds and survive her deadly disease. Ed was by Theresa's side day in and day out, unable to work. He stood by, helpless as his wife and youngest daughter seemed to be rapidly slipping away from him, and the bills just kept piling up.

The prognosis for granulomatosis was dismal; 80 percent of the patients died within a year, 90 percent within two years.

The newspaper mentioned that a few community groups, businesses, and churches were collecting donations for Theresa and her children. *Their efforts were a good start,* I thought, *but not nearly enough, with funds trickling in too slowly.*

The article overwhelmed me. Such a compounded crisis was a truly unimaginable situation. My heart ached for the Schmitt family; I felt their anguish and burden on a very deep level, as if it were my very own.

The columnist said that Southeast Christian Church had been helping the stricken family by covering the insurance premiums for the children. I was a member of that same congregation of several thousand members, and had recently completed training to become a commissioned volunteer care minister. Prior to learning about the Schmitt family, I had been contemplating what my first assignment would be, as all of the new care ministry volunteers would be doing. The timing of completing that training just as I learned about the Schmitts and of all the events in my life that first had to bring me to that point was remarkable. My spiritual and emotional connection to this family's crisis was no accident. So the following day, I decided to call and learn more about what was being done for the Schmitt family.

Mike Graham, the church administrator, helped me put things into perspective on providing relief for this stricken family.

I told Mike, "I want to do something to help but don't know what they need."

"Sharon, they need all the help they can get, and I'm sure the family would appreciate anything you can do."

Our prayers went out to this painfully stressed family, and Mike's encouragement clarified for me exactly what I needed to do, but I had no idea how. Now I had to find the strength, time, and energy to carry out some of my extravagant ideas.

I made my heartfelt and enthusiastic commitment before God to help them, but with such an overwhelming task, where was I to start? I realized I had to talk to Ed to find out their most pressing needs, and decided to go to the hospital.

The following Monday, I anxiously called the church to learn where Theresa was hospitalized. Chuck Lee, another Southeast minister, answered the phone.

"Hello Chuck, this is Sharon Stevens."

It took him a moment to place me. "Well, hello, Sharon. How are you?"

"Fine, thank you, but I'm trying to find a way to help the Schmitt family."

"Yes, I see," he murmured as if something was wrong. He then added mournfully, "Sharon, are you aware that Theresa died yesterday morning? We just found out ourselves."

I was taken totally aback at the news of Theresa's death. My heart sank; the thought of being too late to help her sickened me.

"Oh, no," I replied tearfully. "I was determined to do something to help all of them."

Immediately Chuck responded softly, "Sharon, the children need you now, more than ever. Their problems are many, and they're alone with a very wounded father."

Those few effective words brought me back to what my commitment was about: the special needs of those little girls. I knew what it meant to lose a mother. Perhaps Michelle was too young to understand, but Ashley would be old enough to grieve the loss of her mother deeply. I was willing to do whatever I could to alleviate this family from any more pain.

After my talk with Chuck, I found Theresa's obituary in the morning paper. She was just twenty-nine years old when she died. I decided to attend the visitation the next day to connect with the family. I wanted them to know that they weren't alone, and that I was going to help them in any way I could.

The next day at the funeral home, I first approached the girls' grandmother, Barbara Schmitt. Barbara looked at me with curiosity.

"Mrs. Schmitt, my name is Sharon Stevens. I read the article in the newspaper about your family's misfortunes and would like to do something to help out."

Barbara smiled and thanked me. She looked exhausted and worried. "I don't know what we're going to do. My husband was getting ready to retire, and now he can't. And we have to help Ed raise these two young children."

Barbara seemed to appreciate my concern and offer of support, but she was still in shock and couldn't gauge the sincerity of my offer. I asked Barbara if I could contact her later to learn more about the family's immediate needs. She agreed and thanked me for my discretion.

Ed stepped over, and Barbara introduced me. I told him of my intentions to help out, and he was also appreciative, but he must have been deluged at the time by well-wishers who didn't follow through. My actions would have to speak for me.

By now, Barbara's eyes were red and puffy from tearing up, and Ed paced nervously, struggling to hold his composure as he greeted the long line of friends, neighbors, and strangers like me. I told them I would be in touch and stepped over to the open casket.

Theresa was so young and pretty, lying peacefully surrounded by flowers whose scent wafted through the room. The children were not in the room; they were too young and vulnerable to be exposed to any illness, with all the commotion of people coming and going.

The following day I attended Theresa's funeral service, along with a large turnout from the whole community. I remembered my mother's and father's sparsely attended funerals. Yes, I could relate to this family's tragedy, and was glad so many had come to comfort them.

I did not approach Barbara or Ed at the funeral. The last thing they needed at this time was another stranger talking to them. As

I drove home, it was not my parents' funerals I thought about, but my uncle's death, and the stranger I met as my aunt was making her husband's funeral arrangements.

6

Brick by Brick

1955

One of life's great spiritual questions is "Why do bad things happen to good people?" This is particularly puzzling when it involves innocent children.

Finding God's plan for us sometimes takes us down tormenting paths. To learn compassion, we often must first experience our own suffering. Yes, suffering is painful and often leaves us with more questions than answers, but as they say, the strongest steel is forged by intense fire.

Some of the most harrowing episodes of my childhood made me stronger in the end. They enabled me to forgive, to let go of the hate that would drain my precious energy, and to find understanding instead. From the crossroads of forgiveness, I could finally set out to fulfill the many missions God had for me, and become whole and loving again. But while I was in the middle of it, I had to find a different kind of strength and courage.

• • •

As I MENTIONED previously, when I was very young, my parents would bring me with them on their drinking binges. I would spend hours upon hours huddled in the back of the bar on a stool, curled up in a booth, alone in the car or outside, exposed to everyone else who came to drink. The first time I was taunted and threatened by a stranger I was a young child at one of those bars, clutching my baby doll, and very aware my parents were not going to protect me.

My parents treated me like a possession or a servant rather than their own flesh and blood, and soon enough I would learn why.

I was about nine years old when I was sent north to Indiana to spend time with acquaintances of my parents. I was to help this family during a grave illness, doing household chores and tending to a bedridden man.

My parents had several drinking buddies, but this couple was more colorful than most, and I liked them. The four of them spent many weekends together carrying on like children, drinking and laughing about their many mishaps and even near escapes with death. They had done this for many years.

I had called this couple "Auntie and Uncle" for as long as I could remember. Uncle always teased me and sometimes played practical jokes on me. Auntie would sit back, drinking another beer and laughing at my naïve and childish trust in one of her husband's many pranks.

Once, he dressed me up in disguise and sent me out "snipe hunting" all day. My silly scarecrow costume and the mustache he had drawn on my lip with a ballpoint pen would hide my real identity from the snipes, I was told.

So I went out into the neighborhood hunting snipes, hiding behind bushes and sneaking around corners, but I never found one. A neighbor, who saw me dressed in this hideous garb and carrying around a big paper bag, came out to see why I was dressed that way. I proudly explained that I was snipe hunting for my uncle and that they would run away if they saw me chasing after them.

The neighbor shook his head and burst out laughing at the joke that Uncle had played on me. I was confused by his reaction and figured he was just clueless about snipe hunting. Eventually, the kids in the neighborhood, knowing Uncle's penchant for practical jokes, set me straight.

This older couple never had children of their own, and they treated me as part of their own extended family. They were generally kind to me and looked after me when I was in their care. But I would soon encounter my first two childhood crises at their home in Indiana.

I was sent to stay a week with them. Uncle had been sick with kidney cancer for some time and was no longer able to work. He and Auntie owned a restaurant, and while she was at work, she needed help to care for Uncle.

I was glad to help him out. He was a lot of fun to be around, and Uncle had always been very good to me. I was able to bring him his medication an d warm up a lunch that Auntie had fixed for him. I helped him to the bathroom, then back into his bed. I would read to him during the day when we weren't watching television.

Uncle told me that I was "the best nurse in the whole wide world." He was a pleasant and grateful patient, and I really liked tending to him. But after three days of constant care, unbeknown to me, Uncle began to hemorrhage internally, putting my nine-year-old abilities to a dramatic test.

I immediately called Auntie to tell her of Uncle's worsening condition, and then I hurried back to his bed to comfort him as best I could. Uncle grasped my small hand, looked up at me, and smiled. Then he said softly, "Thank you, sweetheart, for being here for me," and drifted away, losing consciousness.

I continued to hold his hand, speaking softly and lovingly to him. I wasn't sure if he could hear me. I was still holding his cold, moist hand when Auntie arrived and pulled his hand off of me. She called the hospital. I was so confused.

When I saw the big, white ambulance arrive, I thought that Uncle would really like driving away in it with the sirens blasting and red lights blaring. But the ambulance drove off silently, taking Uncle to the morgue and not to an operating room at the hospital.

Auntie had to make arrangements for the funeral and take care of all the details that follow when your spouse dies. I am sure she called my parents, but it would be a long while before they would arrive. She had arranged for Uncle's brother Joe to stay with me until her return. Somehow, she thought I was old enough to care for a dying man by myself, but not old enough to stay at her house alone. Once Auntie had left, Joe abruptly told me, "Go to your room and lie down."

I was startled, not accustomed to taking naps at age nine, but did as I was told. After lying there thinking about Uncle and wondering what had become of him, I eventually fell asleep. Not long after, Joe came into the room and lay down.

Today, many children have been told about personal space, inappropriate touching, and what to do if someone makes them feel threatened. Children today are taught to say no, to yell, fight back, run, and tell someone, but in 1955, at nine years old, I had no idea what was happening. Frightened, I pulled away from him and pretended not to pay attention to what he was doing to me. I then asked to go outside to play.

With an angry, deep voice, he snapped, "Go on! Get out of here," and he called me a vulgar name.

I ran outside, deeply frightened, and in shock. I didn't have words for what had happened to me, but I knew it wouldn't have happened if other adults were home. I stared down the road, desperate to see Auntie's car, and kept looking back to see where Joe was.

About half an hour later, he came outside and walked toward me. He said in a harsh tone, "Sharon! Get in the car."

I knew I was in serious danger but was too afraid of him to disobey. Today, a child would hopefully have the courage to run to the neighbors, but it is hard when we are taught to obey our elders. When I got in his car, he drove to a deserted park and pulled to the side of the road.

I continued staring out the window, my heart pounding from fright, but I dared not look him in the face, trying to be brave. He reached over, and again, I had no idea what to do. I was frantic and tremendously intimidated by his adult size. I finally couldn't hold back my tears any longer.

I turned my head toward Joe and looked him straight in the eyes. My lips quivering, I sobbed, "I want to go home now."

He stopped touching me, reached into the glove compartment, and handed me a Kleenex to dry my tears. He then started the car and drove us back to Auntie's house. On the way, he stopped to buy me an ice-cream cone.

When we arrived back at Auntie's, I stayed outside, blaming my melting ice-cream cone as an excuse to stay out of his reach. I was unaware that Auntie had come home and was busy inside.

Immediately, Auntie came out to me, wanting to make sure I was all right after my deathbed experience with Uncle. Of course, she was unaware that I had been molested by her brother-in-law.

"Sharon, I just want to thank you so much for being here with Clarence, and that he didn't die alone."

This was the first time I had heard Uncle called by name. "He was very sweet to me in the end," I said, my heart still pounding from the threat that waited for me just inside the house.

A tear rolled down her cheek. "You know we love you like our own child, Sharon."

Auntie recovered and glanced over at my ice-cream cone. "Wasn't that nice of Uncle Joe to take you out and buy you an ice cream?"

I almost choked on my last bite but remained silent. Uncle's death was already too much for Auntie to take, and I didn't have the heart, or the courage, to tell her what had happened to me.

I thought about when, or if, I should tell anyone about Joe. I was afraid to say anything for several reasons: I feared that no one would believe me. If they did believe me, I was afraid my parents would be mad at Auntie, and it might cause a rift between them, when she needed them the most. And I was afraid of Joe. So I kept this secret to myself.

Once my parents entered Auntie's home later that day, Joe couldn't get away fast enough. During their visit with Auntie, only my mother's sniffles could be heard among the serious, soft-spoken conversation about Uncle and his life and what he meant to all of them.

As we left Auntie's house and headed for Kentucky, it was only then that I felt safe from Joe's reach. As we drove onto the bridge to Kentucky, the crossover put this experience in the past as a secret I would hold for years.

This incident was not the first time I had been frightened in such a way, and it wouldn't be the last. All of those experiences built up a wall within me, brick by brick.

If you experienced sexual abuse, recently or as a child, don't let it define or hold you back. Like Sharon, you may not have had words for it when it happened, but now you do. Don't assume you are "over it." Help is available, and healing is possible. Resources are available in the back of the book.

7

Bombshell

1958 (1993)

As time passed, our family life soon started to change. Mother's constant drinking began causing more problems at home as I bore the brunt of the anger that she inflicted on us.

Her once kind and gentle spirit now was marked by drastic mood swings almost every day. Coming home from school, I didn't know who I would meet: my once caring and loving mother or the Mad Hatter from *Alice's Adventures in Wonderland*. To say the least, it was a confusing and insecure time for me.

And then I got hit with a bombshell, the most shocking thing I had ever experienced in my life—a secret my parents apparently planned to keep from me forever. I was twelve years old. It all started with an innocent kindness.

That morning, I woke up to a damp, gloomy school day. After eating breakfast, I grabbed a raincoat from the closet. Clutching my book bag, I headed out the door to walk to school. That day, Dad was leaving for work at the same time, and dropped me off.

My classes went along as usual, but toward the end of the day, an extraordinary and ferocious storm arose suddenly, just as school let out. The thunder rumbled, the lighting cracked, and the sky filled with dark rolling clouds.

Many concerned parents drove to the school to pick up their children who lived nearby and walked home. My mother did not know how to drive, and we only had one car, which Dad drove to work every day, leaving me to manage as best I could.

I headed out to the street to make my way home. The violent wind and rain bent the trees back and forth, and I jumped in fear as a lightning bolt struck nearby, the winds blowing rain pellets like needles into my face. I dreaded the long walk ahead of me but continued pushing forward.

As I hurried along, trying unsuccessfully to keep my rain hood in place, a carload of neighborhood kids pulled over, driven by the teenage son of one of my parents' friends. They offered me a safe ride home out of the storm, but I wasn't allowed to get into cars with other kids. This was one of the many rules my parents had for me that kept me as isolated as possible. The friends seemed genuinely concerned about my safety as the rain pelted my skin and lightning flashed around us. The group insisted, and so I accepted the ride.

As we got closer to my house, I explained that my mother would be furious if she found out I had ridden home in their car. I asked them to let me out about a block away from my house, explaining I would run home from there. They understood my request, knowing that my parents were very strict.

As the door opened for me to get out of the old car, two boys sitting in the front had to step out first, so I could push the seat forward from the back. I thanked them and hurried for home, thinking everything was all right.

But a neighbor had seen me, called my mother, and told her she saw me get out of a car full of boys. The implied impropriety was a very dangerous message to deliver to my alcoholic mother. The damage this meddling person caused would change my life forever, infuriating my mother to the point of destroying what remained of our rocky relationship. After this incident and what followed, I would lose whatever sense of family I had left, and would become an outsider from that moment on.

When I entered the house, my mother stood there waiting for me, hands on her hips. It was apparent that she had been drinking as usual, but today she was more outraged than I had ever seen her.

Unaware of what was fueling her anger, I remained silent and let her lead the way. Her piercing eyes smoldered with hatred—or was it disgust? She told me of the neighbor's phone call.

Mom violently spit out, "You're going to be a tramp, just like your mother." She jabbed her finger into my face, shaking it furiously at me.

I stepped back, trembling and confused. "Mom, what are you saying?"

She repeated her indictment. "I said, you are going to be a tramp just like your mother, and start causing us problems. And *that* I'm not going to tolerate! Do you hear me?"

Baffled, I shouted back, "I only rode home with those kids because of the storm. A lightning bolt almost struck me; I could've been killed! Don't you even care about that?"

"Of course, but I'd rather see you die than be a tramp!"

I was totally lost by this accusation, her words "just like your mother" piercing my heart. What was she telling me?

After a sip of her beer, she went on to say, "You have bad genes from your mother."

There, I thought. *She said it again.* My head was spinning. I asked, "Mom? What are you telling me? If you aren't my mother, then who is?"

She turned and glared at me and said, "Anna's your real mother! You hear that, tramp? You're no blood kin to me!"

I was in total shock hearing this revelation. I started shaking and had to lean against the wall for fear of collapsing.

At first I couldn't recall who Anna was, but moments later it registered. A woman named Anna visited my parents from time to time and was the daughter of one of my father's best friends. I remembered that she once babysat me, and I cried the whole time. She had four daughters, who I enjoyed playing with when she visited our home.

Mom offered no further explanation and took another sip of her beer, still glaring at me. I had to get to the bottom of this shocking news. Anna was my biological mother? Instantly, my entire life became a question mark. Why did she abandon me? Why did this couple adopt me?

I finally had to step into the living room and sit down. Imagine thinking you know who you are one minute and then finding out that you're not that person, and then being accused of having "bad genes"—my thoughts were whirling.

My mind quickly ran through a reel of every memory I had

of Anna and her girls. What struck me most about Anna was her kindness and those wonderful peals of laughter. I loved how she played with her pretty, young daughters. There was nothing about her to suggest Mom's accusation that she was some sort of harlot. Anna's life seemed beautiful and happy. Surely, she could see that my life had been full of neglect and instability. Why didn't she rescue me? I had many other questions about my life that needed answers, and I was going to ask them. I deserved to know the truth.

As I sat on the couch, my mother retreated into the back of the house. I went to the phone in the kitchen, where Mom kept her phone book. I scanned through it until I found an Anna Pritchard at a nearby address. I dialed Anna's number, just as big as you please. I had no idea what I would say to her, but as an impulsive twelve-year-old, I wanted answers, she had them, and that was that.

The phone rang twice before a sweet, gentle voice answered. I thought I recognized Anna's voice.

I said without hesitation, "Is this Anna?"

She asked, "Yes, it is. Who am I speaking with?"

I said rather abruptly, "This Is Sharon Boman." I paused for a moment, then blurted out my question. "My mother just told me that she's not my mother, but that you are. Is this true?"

This moment must have been tense for Anna, and there was a brief silence. Anna knew nothing of why this secret had suddenly been disclosed, but she responded very gently and calmly. "Yes, Sharon. It is true." She paused, then asked, "Is everything all right there?"

I was stunned. With tears rolling down my face, I said, "No, it's not."

"Okay. Then I think that I'd better come to get you so that we can talk. I would like that. Wouldn't you?"

This was the offer I desperately needed to hear from her. "Would you, please? I am very confused right now."

I didn't understand why this had been such a big secret. My parents had taught me to be open and honest, but I knew I couldn't talk about their drinking. There were a lot of things I kept to myself. To them, honesty did not mean I could say how I felt. I wasn't to give any opinions, only trust them and accept their word as the truth.

Why wouldn't they want me to know about Anna? What else were they keeping from me?

I was confused. My thoughts became jumbled and my stomach flipped as I thought through scenes from my life: their erratic behavior while under the influence, the dangerous situations they put me in, the way they restricted my every move and cut me short when I did something that threatened their lifestyle. Now, within just a few minutes, I yearned to find my own way to a peaceful life.

• • •

ALL OF THIS was happening to me just as I was entering adolescence. For the first time, I was making friends at school and experiencing aspects of life other than their drunken carousing. I loved my parents but knew I could only exist in their life of alcoholism doing things their way. Alcoholism demands every part of you, then spills out to claim your family. Being the child of two alcoholics had swallowed me up, but now, I was beginning to see things clearly. I wanted to be happy, and at the same time, my natural teenage mindset was also emboldening me to take some control back of this life I had been living in the shadow of alcoholism.

The chaos of my parents' drinking brought many painful problems I still live with today, but it also taught me independence and gave me courage. Now, everything was coming to a head.

Learning about my adoption abruptly stripped me of my identity; I became deeply angry with my parents, who had deceived me all this time, who had failed to protect me, who had deliberately thrust me into dangerous environments over and over as if I was an inconvenience, or a piece of property that others could borrow whenever they needed. Living with alcoholic parents forced me to be the adult in the household when I was just a child, taking care of them, cleaning up after them, covering for them, and taking care of myself as well. Now, I was in full rebellion. This situation pushed me to want to become truly independent, and the revelations of my adoption gave me incentive to allow my hidden identity to rise and to become the person I always wanted to be.

At twelve, I had to make an adult decision to break away and direct my life toward a different, more loving culture than the drunkenness and abuse of my present family life. I had only my self-respect and moral sense of things to carry me through this oppressive, sensitive period.

The confusion this created caused a turmoil of undeserved frustration within me, and inflicted heightened emotions on me far beyond the natural hormonal swings of adolescence. I was hollow and empty inside, but outside, in my home, things were getting worse and worse, forcing me to cope with delicate situations that no gangly preteen should have to endure. I wanted to run from those situations—and from my parents as well.

8

Ask for the Moon

AUGUST–SEPTEMBER 1992

Thirty years later, I understood what it meant to lose a mother, to be in a position where you had to grow up far too soon. Of course, my situation was far different, and Ashley was only three—Michelle, just two. The shock of discovering that I was adopted could not compare to what the girls must be feeling. To be living under your mother's constant loving care, and then for her to disappear from your life suddenly, would be terribly traumatic, especially for Ashley, who still needed very specialized care following her liver transplant.

Theresa was hospitalized for several weeks before she passed on, and was fairly unresponsive during those last few weeks of her life. And because of her compromised system, Ashley couldn't visit her mother in the hospital at the end. Theresa died just after Ashley began to recover from receiving her new liver.

For Michelle, losing her mother might affect her will to thrive, a condition that could easily affect her ability to survive long enough to receive her own liver transplant. Now just twenty months old, Michelle had not spoken a word, other than small grunts of "yes" and "no."

I thought about the added trauma these sweet little lambs were facing as I exited the church after Theresa's funeral. I couldn't take away such a heavy loss, but I could help in more tangible ways to ease their burden. It was time for me to act.

I took a look at what resources I had, and what I knew how to do. By this time, I was a successful hair designer with many well-known clients. My shop was on the first floor of a prominent hotel in the east end of Louisville. My first fundraising idea was to hold a hair-a-thon. I decided I would gather a group of hairdressers to cut hair and donate the money to our cause. Hairdressers are, as a rule, a very selfless bunch; I figured local stylists would want to participate, and they did. Besides my group, hairdressers from all over town joined in.

You may think, how could a bunch of hairdressers ever think they could make a dent in such a great need? Why would this woman, this hairstylist, even attempt such a thing? But, think about it. Everyone needs a haircut. From the richest, most powerful people to the people who work their fingers to the bone in manual jobs, everyone eventually ends up sitting in a salon or barber's chair. We take care of them, give them a moment of rest, make them feel more confident, and listen to them. We know people. Lots of people. So, why *not* a hairstylist, a *group* of hairstylists, to get things done?

I set the date for the end of the next month and got to work. In terms of publicity, I couldn't afford to do more than design and put out flyers. However, I did spend a lot of time on the phone, contacting the media to let the public know the details, and reached out to the mayor's office.

I needed more specific information from the family to set a legitimate fundraising goal. I wanted to be able to explain to donors how we would use this money, and why it was so desperately needed. I called Barbara to let her know what we were planning. She understood and began to list their outstanding debt and what was needed to provide Michelle with a new liver. Then Barbara invited me to their home to meet Ashley and Michelle for the first time.

I drove over on a beautiful day, anxious to meet the children. I had only seen their black-and-white newspaper photos, which were sorrowful and heartbreaking. I couldn't imagine the effect their actual presence would have on me.

Ashley's transplant had taken place the year before, and she was recuperating very nicely, but I had to wonder about Michelle. Would she be too sick to interact with me? Would she find my presence stressful? On top of her being ill, strangers probably upset her, having doctors and nurses prodding and poking her constantly. She might not welcome another person into her life, even if she could understand I was there to help.

I arrived and walked up to the front door of their lovely but modest home. As Barbara opened the door and greeted me, I could smell the aroma of coffee and freshly baked cinnamon rolls. As I stepped inside, Ashley shyly peeked around the corner to observe me, no doubt wondering who this woman was.

Behind her, Michelle looked over her sister's shoulder. I smiled and waved my hand in greeting. They looked absolutely precious, dressed in pastel ruffles with bows in their hair. As I followed Barbara into the living room, I got a better look at these innocent children who had suffered so much.

The girls were very well behaved, despite their constant medical problems. Their eyes peered through me as if their souls were also taking a peek into my heart. Like falling in love at first sight, I immediately knew the "rightness" of my mission to help these children any way I could.

Ashley was curious about me. "Hi," she said as she came toward me. "I'm Ashley. Who are you?"

I squatted down to her eye level. "I'm a friend here to help. My name is Sharon."

Ashley nodded her head. "*Share-run.*" She smiled. "That's my sister, Michelle."

Michelle scooted behind her grandmother, peeking out at me from behind her wide skirt, never saying a word.

Barbara had me sit on one couch while she and the girls sat across from me on another. I could easily see and compare Ashley's condition, one year after her transplant surgery, to Michelle, in desperate need of a new liver. The difference was obvious and spurred me on.

Ashley looked amazingly healthy. Her hair shone, her eyes were bright and sparkling, and her cheeks were rosy. She had a quick mind for a child just under four years old. She watched my every move and listened carefully to everything I said.

On the other hand, Michelle appeared weak and tired, even this early in the day. Her skin color was jaundiced, and her little tummy hung over her waist, bloated by her enlarged liver. She had scratch marks and scabs all over her body from the constant itching caused by her condition.

Her beautiful, sad eyes struck me. She was miserably sick and no doubt suffered greatly, and yet I sensed that she never complained. I wondered if this little one understood something the rest of us often forget: that our life is on loan to us, and we should be grateful for every moment we live.

Michelle was about twenty months old but weighed only eleven pounds. Her tiny hands were the size of a newborn baby's. That morning she hid behind her grandmother with her pacifier in her mouth but never took her eyes off of me. Sometimes children see more than what adults can understand. What was she seeing in me?

As I talked with Barbara and got updates on their debts and the cost of Michelle's surgery, Ashley disappeared into her room and returned with her favorite toys for me to see. She told me her dolls' names, showed me her yellow truck and her puzzles. While Michelle hung back, Ashley and I became fast friends.

Barbara sat with me for hours, pouring out their family story, filling in what the newspaper article had left out. Their situation was more critical than I had ever imagined. As their debts accumulated, some companies wanted assurances that they could pay it off, leaving them in fear about being denied future care, or losing their home.

I found that the family was responsible for 20 percent of the overall costs. Ashley's surgery was $400,000. The liver itself was $25,000, and was not covered by insurance. Theresa's hospital bill came to over $600,000 for the intensive care and life support she received before her death.

The children's medication was costly. Ashley's was $600 a month at the time, and she would need it for the rest of her life. Michelle's medication was $1,000 a month, which would increase before her surgery. Neither could survive without it, and the state paid only $400 a month for both of them. Then, there was the cost of getting Michelle to Nebraska for surgery, and for family housing during her hospitalization, not to mention the never-ending medical complications these girls would face in their lifetime. A million dollars would still not be enough to keep this family financially stable through Ashley's and Michelle's childhoods.

Thankfully, I was not alone in my calling to help this family. As it turned out, hearts were breaking for them throughout the city, thanks to the same article I read and a follow-up report about Theresa's death. God was sprouting angels' wings on ordinary people well beyond the state of Kentucky, each one destined to play their part. Some would play just a small role, and some, it turned out, would make huge sacrifices to help these girls.

All I knew, though, all I could think about, was what *I* was called to do. As far as I knew at the time, it was up to me and as many other angels as I could muster to tackle these gigantic obstacles. It became apparent that my fundraising efforts would need to increase substantially. I showed Barbara the flyer with the children's pictures on it. Ashley was proud to see her picture there. Barbara was grateful for the participation of all of these hairdressers from across the city.

Michelle just stared at her picture, no doubt wondering what it all meant. Barbara was grateful that something was being done, no matter its size. As she walked me to the door, she said, "I don't know how I can ever repay you for what you're doing."

I looked past Barbara and smiled at the children trailing behind her. "Your job is to take good care of these babies." I then added rather gallantly, "Let me worry about raising money to pay the bills." As I drove away, I did wonder if that was possible. In fact, if I were a person who knew more about such things, I would have realized raising that kind of money was truly an impossible goal. Thankfully, I didn't know enough to have that kind of skepticism.

I was delighted I had met with them. Seeing the girls motivated me, and Barbara had given me a broad overview of their financial situation. The next morning, I created a strategy. There are two ways to cover expenses: raise money, and lower costs. We would need to do both. I believed we would raise the money, but this family needed more than that. I made my first call to set up a jet team alliance to ensure the family had a jet ready to transport Michelle when the call came for her surgery.

I had never asked for anything in my life, but I would ask for the moon for Michelle. As I sat with the phone in front of me, I tried to figure out who to call and what to say. I needed a jet to be ready with only a six-hour window to get Michelle airborne and on her way to Omaha, and I wanted them to cut the price drastically.

After taking a deep breath, I called the first airline company and asked to speak directly to the president. I was immediately transferred to his executive secretary, a woman named Katie. She was very kind and concerned about Michelle's condition.

I explained the family's dire financial situation and that Michelle would die if she didn't get a liver transplant within the next few months. Katie was familiar with the newspaper account of Ashley's surgery.

She put me on hold for a few minutes while she delivered my request to the president. She briefly returned to ask a couple of questions that I readily answered and then came back with his answer. "Yes. Give us a short window of time, and we'll have a plane available at no cost."

I was somewhat astonished by the ease and quickness of their response. Of course, the newspaper coverage of the family's situation and the mother's recent death and funeral seemed to have galvanized the whole Louisville community and beyond. *Perhaps,* I realized, *this task really is possible.*

But I needed more than one airline's commitment, given that the call could come at any time. So I continued calling other airlines and corporations who had private jets, requesting their help. I had set out to get four aircraft on standby, and four is what I got.

Two Louisville-based companies, the KFC Corporation and Pattco, Inc., were particularly passionate about wanting to provide transportation. These people cared about Michelle and her plight from the bottom of their hearts. They constantly called to check on how she was doing and get an update on the availability of a transplant liver for her.

The cost of Theresa's hospital bill was another concern and a great success story. I called the hospital and spoke with the administrator about dismissing or possibly lowering the $600,000 bill. I spent about three days with social workers and the administration, who said they would get back to me after they looked into it further.

Then, within a week, we received letters from the hospital saying that they would drop all out-of-pocket expenses to the family. My heart skipped a beat at this turnaround, which in my mind, made the relief of other debts possible.

I went over to the Schmitts' house to celebrate our small victory. Ashley didn't quite understand it all, but she could see the relief on everybody's faces. She sat next to me and said, "I wish Mom were here."

I took her hand and said, "She's always here, Ashley, looking over you and Michelle. Never forget that." She squeezed my hand.

9

Anna's Choice

1958–1959

Going home that evening, I thought about how a simple phone call could completely change a situation. Ashley's longing for her mother and her grief at losing her reminded me of the call I made to Anna, decades before. Nothing was going to stop me from making that call, when I learned she was my biological mother. Until that time, she had been a distant presence watching over me—only I never knew it.

Anna's response was warm, assuring me that I had no reason to fear a meeting with her. I knew she would answer my questions honestly about my adoption, so I waited patiently for her arrival to pick me up.

I avoided my mother, who I assumed was not aware that Anna was on the way. I feared what she would do to me if she found out I had made that call, assuming she would probably make things worse than they already were.

Remarkably, she reacted as if it was not a surprise to her when Anna knocked on our door. She was very nice to Anna and gave her approval for us to spend time together at Anna's house.

After greetings, Anna turned to me and said, "Sharon, go put some things in an overnight bag. You're coming to my house for a few days. The girls and I would love to visit with you, and I'm guessing the time away would be good for everyone concerned."

I hurriedly packed a bag and came downstairs. Anna opened the door for me, and Mom practically shoved me out. "Be polite, and we'll talk when you get back, Sharon."

As we drove to Anna's big, beautiful home alongside the tranquil setting of a park, I scanned her from head to toe. We looked alike, including our hands and feet. Even our laugh was identical. As we relaxed enough to enjoy these astonishing but precious "first" moments together, I continued studying her intently.

She looked over at me, laughing. "What are you doing?"

"We look just alike, don't we?"

Anna said, "Yes, honey. We sure do."

I felt protected, knowing that my birth mother was close by and cared for me. Throughout those years of chaotic and trying episodes Mom and Daddy had put me through, I knew someday I would somehow find peace. In this moment, I felt that my belated reunion with Anna would provide a pathway. I was, for the moment, blissfully unaware that this would not be the case.

Anna spent the entire evening explaining the circumstances of my birth and her reasons for giving me to the Bomans. She was just a teenager, she explained, and there was no way she could raise me. Because of religious reasons, she could not get an abortion, nor would she.

I could tell from her patient explanation that giving me up hurt her, too. It wasn't just her words, but her sad eyes that expressed the pain she felt, then and now. I wanted to comfort her, to give her some affection in return for what she was giving me at that moment.

I scooted over on the couch and gave her a big hug. We both teared up. I felt lucky to have found the birth mother I didn't even know I was missing, to fill a void in my life I never before understood. We quickly developed a bond that comforted me like nothing I had experienced in my life.

We discussed my adopted mother's feelings. Anna was very concerned for her well-being as well. I told her about the heavy drinking, but Anna could not believe it, sure that I was exaggerating. Anna had never seen my mother drunk on her visits to our house nor noticed any deterioration of her mental health.

Despite the pain that my adopted mother had inflicted on me, I didn't want to hurt her. Until that moment, she was the only mother

I had ever known. As is common for family members of alcoholics, I even made excuses for her, and reasoned that I was the cause of her drinking. *To keep a secret like my adoption, always wondering when I would find out and what my reaction would be, must have put a lot of pressure on her,* I told myself.

Anna urged me to appreciate the Bomans for being there for me all of those years. She assured me that my adoptive mother loved me very much, and she advised me to consider how hard it would be to be separated from someone you love. I never told Anna the details about the life I had been living, taking care of my parents, being put in difficult and dangerous situations, being kept isolated. This life was all I knew, and it didn't occur to me that anyone needed to know, particularly since my parents had drilled into me not to talk about my family; I was just beginning to realize mine had not been a "normal" life for a little girl.

Anna admitted that the Bomans were too strict with me, but assured me, naively, that as I got older this would get better. We arranged for me to visit her on weekends, and I thought this could be the remedy for all of us. I looked forward to these plans very much.

I hung on to Anna's every word, trying to make sense of everything, and adored her for being such a kind, considerate person. She was everything I had imagined in a mother, and I was thrilled to now have her in my life.

My weekend soon ended, and it was hard for me to walk away from Anna, but I was anxious to see my adoptive parents. I hoped that this revelation had lessened the pressure on Mom and that, perhaps, she would stop drinking.

I wanted to balance my two families evenly, taking precautions not to hurt anybody's feelings. I assumed this trait was something I inherited from my birth mother, and perhaps it was. But I would come to learn that family members of alcoholics often put themselves under pressure to make sure everyone is happy, working themselves to death to keep the peace.

As we headed home, I was still a little afraid of what I was walking into at the Bomans' house, the only home I had ever known. Mom's drinking and mood swings were tough to live with. Would they let up now? I did look forward to being with my father, who considered me his pride and joy. I hoped that we had all learned to be kinder to each other after this incident.

My father's warm smile greeted me as I entered the house. Mom was cooking dinner, my favorite, and I went off to clean up. We carried on at dinner as if nothing had changed. No mention was made of Anna and her family or of the incident that had triggered our confrontation. We entered into a period of uneasy peace, not talking about what we desperately needed to share.

• • •

I CONTINUED TO visit my birth mother and her family from time to time, and I enjoyed my new half-sisters very much. Not only did I gain four sisters, but two of them were a set of twins who had adventurous spirits.

My oldest sister was a teenager a few years older than me. She loved rock-and-roll records, boys, and clothes—all the things teenagers liked. I had not developed such interests yet. In a few years, I would learn the ropes of "how to catch a boyfriend" from her.

The twins were a different story. We all shared an interest in athletics and games. In the summer, we swam every day at a pool close to their home. At night we would sit around talking about anything and everything, laughing the whole night long. One twin was very sweet-natured and always had a soft smile; she was kind-hearted like our mother. The other twin was robust and rambunctious, overpowering almost everyone around her. She said whatever came to her mind and could be a bully, but one look from her sister would undercut her belligerence.

My youngest sister was a loner and stayed out of everyone's way. She was more independent than the others and was a tomboy just like me. We also shared some adventures and had the closeness of best friends. We had a secret bond, one we both needed as misfits in the world. She turned out to be the prettiest of us all, and the most self-sufficient too.

The more time I spent with Anna's family, the more distant I became with my adoptive parents. I held on to a hope that I would become a part of Anna's family, that she would take me back, dreaming that we would all live together in their beautiful, loving home. At the Bomans, our strained relationship made me feel stressed and alone every day; I wasn't so lonely when I was with my sisters. I asked Anna if I could become a part of her family again and live there all of the time. Unfortunately, this plea would become a turning point in my relationship with my sisters and would separate us once again.

"It's not that I don't *want* you," she told me. "I'm just afraid of hurting the Bomans. They stepped in and helped me when I was in need. There is so much to consider in this situation. Mostly, I just don't want to inflict emotional pain on anybody."

Nobody but me, I knew inside.

I admired Anna's gentleness, and was not surprised at her rejection of my request to live with her. I came to think of myself the way I had been treated all my life; as a nuisance and an inconvenience. I never truly expected anyone to put me first in their lives. How much my adoptive mother loved and looked out for me depended on her level of intoxication in that moment. The more drunk she became, the more her fear and bitterness took over. How much Anna loved me would come down to reputation, and the wishes of her other daughters.

Anna was involved in ministry, and my presence in her life threatened that work. If people knew about me, she feared, she would be shamed and not permitted to continue her work for the church. I wanted her to be happy and especially not feel shameful about me, not feel ashamed *of* me. The more I became aware of this conflict, the more I knew I needed to go on with my life separately, sparing everyone any grief. Somehow, just as I felt I was responsible for my mother's drinking, I felt responsible for Anna's shame, another by-product of being raised in an alcoholic home.

In time the bold twin told me bluntly to get out of their lives. She felt that I was a skeleton in the closet that would tarnish the family's name. The sisters all wanted to raise Christian children and shelter them from their mother's past mistake, I was told, and they couldn't do that with me around them.

This sister would never seem to realize or care about how she hurt me with her cutting words and misplaced fears. Her words shattered every hope I had to be a part of what I felt belonged to me, of what I needed so desperately, and none of the others seemed to disagree with her, as no one reached out to me after that. I assumed that she spoke for the others, and I accepted her rejection. I walked out of their lives almost as quickly as I entered.

As an adult, I turned away from Christianity for years because I believed I was someone the church would be ashamed of. My life was far from perfect; the last place I wanted to be was somewhere I would be judged. It took years to realize she was only one voice among the many Christian believers who take Christ's words to heart: "He that is without sin among you, let him first cast a stone at her."

Time would eventually heal this wounded relationship decades later, but with all things considered, and still reeling from the sting of yet another rejection, I turned my heart back to my home with the Bomans. By this time, my parents were becoming jealous of my relationship with Anna and her family. Perhaps Anna was right; I decided to make the best of what I had with them and spare everyone any further pain. Everyone but me.

10

Genesis

1958–1960

While returning to the Bomans wasn't what I wanted, I had no choice. I felt rejected by one family and diabolically controlled by another. This was all about *their* happiness, regardless of how I felt or what was best for me. My birth mother chose to remain blissfully unaware of how the Bomans treated me. She stepped aside and buried any concern she may have had for my welfare. She and her family were free of me.

Deep inside, I was hurting—but outwardly I showed little of it. Though I had a house to live in and food to eat, I was alone once again, far away from the only protection I had found.

I could not bring myself to blame my birth mother for turning away from me again. *Surely it was my fault,* I told myself. I was to blame. And now, once again, I was an unwilling performer in the Bomans' three-ring circus.

The Bomans' irrational, unreasoned behaviors and reckless carelessness seemed to pick up without missing a beat once I stopped visiting my birth family. This instability continued to create distrust in me, distorting my recently gained confidence. After settling back with them, I started losing all hope of surviving my chaotic home life.

Trying to figure out who I was while battling my adoptive mother's false perception of me as a tainted young woman was challenging at best. My mother's fearful accusations and drunken revelation had led me to my birth mother and gave me a taste of a healthy, loving home. Now, I yearned for freedom, for a new moral compass. I would have to continue that exploration on my own.

Searching for a proper direction without the aid of an adult to guide me or explain why things played out as they did was difficult. I was confused and not ready to trust my own judgment on such matters, but I also knew I couldn't trust the adults around me.

I could only accept the unavoidable fact that I existed in an intricate human web of conflicting aims and desires. I had no choice but to zigzag my way through the havoc that made no sense to me and find my own way.

I did love my adoptive parents and wanted to develop a good relationship with them, but that was not under my control. My world was becoming unbearable for me. There were no siblings to commiserate with, no one who knew my situation, no one to whom I could express my feelings. There were no close friends or relatives, nor were there any new or positive experiences to give me hope. I was alone, disappointed, and ashamed of my many painful secrets.

All along, I feared that my classmates and neighbors would learn about my family and turn away from me; I felt tainted by my parents' sordid behavior. I had already confronted rejection and abandonment from both my adoptive mother and my birth family; I feared a repeat from the local community. So I was cautious about every word I said, careful not to reveal anything about my home situation.

My social restrictions were harsh compared to the other teens my age, designed to hide my parents' alcoholism from view. They only circulated within limited groups of people who shared the same lifestyle. They accepted this drunken world as their life and confined me to it as well. They had no need to worry; the last thing I wanted was for anyone to find out.

I had nothing in common with my parents or their friends. I didn't want to grow up only to drink away my life and hang out with loud, obnoxious people. I wanted to live in a world seemingly unknown to my parents, filled with people contributing to society and helping others.

For the next couple of years, my parents held to their one-sided views and alcoholic lifestyle. As I approached high school, their control tactics caused me no end of disappointment and frustration. An unspoken tension surrounded our lives day after day, making our home cold and rigid.

I was denied all social privileges, like attending sleepovers with my girlfriends in their homes, nor were they allowed to visit our home. In addition, I couldn't attend our school's ball games or dances, even when other teens' parents offered to drive me there and back.

There was absolutely nothing I was allowed to do outside our home other than follow my parents into depressing, smoke-filled taverns and be their designated driver. I certainly was never given the privilege of staying home alone while they went out.

My mother's deep paranoia over my moral character grew far worse, playing out in disturbing ways that left deep emotional scars. My fears of what she would do next grew, as her resentment of me escalated. The more she drank, the more obsessed she became with every move I made. In her mentally ill, alcohol-controlled state, she would inflict painful insults day after day.

In her eyes, I was like a thorn tearing a deep hole in her heart, an embarrassment, and I was sure in my own heart that she regretted ever adopting me. The only way she knew how to deal with her fears was to punish me through her harsh accusations.

And, of course, I was growing into a pretty young woman, my adolescent hormones not making things any easier. I was determined not to allow her to destroy the self-image that I was trying so hard to establish, but I was young, insecure, and like all adolescents, I needed the positive, loving guidance only a mother could provide. I was in search of who I wanted to be deep down inside. So I clung to that, rather than dwell on her fantasies of who she thought I was, or allow her upside-down imaginings to define me.

By the time I was fourteen years old, the abuse had driven me even further away emotionally. Like most families in that era, my father worked hard and left the parenting to my mother. He was not paying attention, and like so many adults, drinking was also part of his daily life. I adored him, but I could not rely on him to help me. A few years later, as a young adult, I would learn that mental illness plagued my adoptive mother's family, and alcohol abuse may have been her attempt to drown out her own descent into that same fate. But her illness did not excuse my father's neglect.

Regardless, I was able to emerge to a degree, finding assurance in the kindness of other mature adults, the parents of school friends. I became more and more independent, surrounding myself whenever I could with positive, successful people from whom to learn—my own small army of secret angels. I became very good at reading people's true character and spotting their hidden motives. I continued to build my own emotional walls of protection and was very careful who I trusted, all the while keeping my own terrible truth hidden.

Looking back, I think this was the genesis of my concern for children with unfulfilled needs and maybe why I responded so fervently to the Schmitt family's problems. At ages four and two, Ashley and Michelle had been severed from the loving, protective care of their mother, and Michelle in particular was in extremely poor health.

My situation growing up was far different, yet still devastating. Perhaps having a chance to help Ashley and Michelle in even a small way could bring some good out of my own loss and abandonment, painful memories that still gripped me thirty years later.

As I began to reach out to the community on behalf of Ashley and Michelle and as their story spread, it seemed everybody wanted to help. I drew on my hard-earned teenage experiences and intuitions about people to weed out those who only wanted to help the girls for their own gain. We would only accept help and participation from people motivated by the right ideals, with no other hidden agendas.

━━━━━

If you recognize or question whether you or a loved one is suffering from a mental or emotional breakdown, there is help and treatment now that was not available decades ago. Resources are provided in the back of this book.

11

Hair-a-Thon

SEPTEMBER 27–28, 1992

The money we raised and the debt that we lowered in a week's time did help, but most of the incoming money went toward medication for the girls. Hopefully, the hair-a-thon would make a big difference. We received an outpouring of interest and participation by local hairdressers.

We called ourselves "The Hair Angels," whose name I later changed to "Angels, Inc." to include everybody else outside our profession who wanted to help. I was proud to organize and represent a group of people who believed in helping others, especially children in dire situations. Deep inside, I was beginning to see something good come out of my own painful childhood; the strength, determination, and compassion I had was born out of those mournful memories. I was no stranger to hard work, but this huge endeavor would require something else I gained from the trauma of my youth: courage.

Still, all of those qualities were not going to be enough. The dozens of hairstylists volunteering their time would not be enough. The task at hand was quickly growing beyond my own abilities. I would need a host of "angels" to join me.

The community-wide hair event was about to take place. Newspaper articles were published, and television and radio news coverage promoted our mission and the children's dire situation. We were becoming known throughout the community. Even Mayor

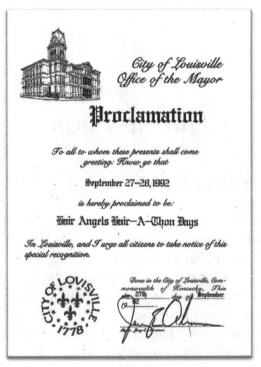

Image courtesy of Sharon Stevens Evans.

Jerry Abramson declared September 27–28, 1992 as "Hair Angels Hair-A-Thon Days."

The general response from people was incredible, joining us in, as one newscaster put it, "the mission of the century" in Louisville, Kentucky, to save the life of this child. Michelle's beautiful but frail image was plastered all over town. I cringed a bit, feeling as if we were exploiting her, but Barbara said Michelle would understand.

I chose to include "angels" in our name because that higher side of our nature comes forth in such cases. And just maybe, I was thinking of the angels who helped me in my own life. In the Bible, angels can't be numbered. They bring messages, listen to God, and carry out his plans. Angels are very powerful, and are always pointing out God's greatness. In my early childhood, certainly I must have had angels protecting me, perhaps preparing me for this very purpose. In my teen years, there were several earthly angels that came to my rescue. Now, the overwhelming response we received from the Louisville community to save Michelle made me realize we had countless angels on the ground, and possibly God had dispatched his heavenly angels to look over us as well.

I soon realized word of our mission was spreading far beyond our city. I got a big surprise and boost when President George H. W. Bush called after reading about our campaign. I gave him some more details about Michelle's liver transplant. He wrote the family a very kind letter, and his office called me and thanked me for helping them.

The hair-a-thon was scheduled to last two days. When the event started, our hairdressers across the city were excited, but we had no idea what to expect. However, we were very busy all day, and everybody was in high spirits. Some of our clients even used the occasion to "try something different" with their hairstyle.

Around 8:00 p.m., the flow of people through our own little shop at the Hurstbourne Hotel and Conference Center slowed down. I told the hairdressers to go home and get some rest for the next day. I remained there just in case someone came by who had been working late. Then at 11:00 p.m., we were featured on the local news, showing us cutting hair to raise money for the children.

From 11:00 p.m. until 3:00 a.m. I was swamped with new customers who had seen the newscast. People came to me before working their late shifts. Out-of-towners poured out of their hotel rooms, some to get haircuts, others just to donate money for Michelle's transplant.

People standing in line in the salon or out on the sidewalk were having a great time. Someone even found an all-night diner and brought me a sandwich. This was one of my most endearing experiences as a hairdresser. I will never forget that night or these caring people, all going out of their way to help a family in need.

The following day my team of hairdressers returned, amazed by the extra money I had raised that night. Customers kept pouring in for haircuts, or just to help out. Later, news trucks showed up to capture Congressman Ron Mazzoli's visit to our shop. Barbara brought Ashley and Michelle over to meet him and to thank the hairdressers, protectively holding Michelle in her arms.

They were dressed as little princesses. Ashley went around and shook everybody's hand and thanked them. The news footage was shown locally that night and picked up on national news feeds. From that day forward, Louisville became, for a while, a shining example for the world of what a caring community could do.

The hair-a-thon was a great success, and the money helped to purchase medication for the children. Yes, you could say it was only a drop in the bucket of what was needed, but drops of water congregate and form oceans. The participation of so many people, along with the media exposure we received, would have a lasting impact. After the event, I would find different ways to raise larger donations for the girls.

Not everyone embraced this selfless endeavor. I was receiving a lot of attention with constant interruptions of my work at the salon. I encountered some resentment and plenty of misjudgment from my fellow stylists, and certainly the extra activities impacted everyone. And, truthfully, when a person is in the middle of carrying out their calling, they feel energized and enjoy it, even if the work is exhausting. I was using gifts and abilities I did not even know I had, and it felt good to be used by God to help someone else. In many ways, my work to bring good health to someone else was bringing healing to me, too. My enthusiasm could easily have been misinterpreted as enjoying the limelight, and I am sure I was carried along by the current of attention for a little while, but for the most part, God and those precious little girls kept my feet on the ground. Finally, I quit and went to another shop, a full-service salon where I had previously worked.

I had been one of their original hairdressers and was anxious to get back among friends. They were interested in and fully supported my fundraising endeavor and were one of the shops that participated in the hair-a-thon. It felt like I was right where I belonged, and I was given the freedom I needed to continue my sometimes intrusive fundraising efforts.

In this first six weeks of work, we had secured a flight for Michelle's surgery, gotten Theresa's hospital bill dismissed, and raised enough hard cash for a month of medication for the girls. All of this support occurred at a time when the family desperately needed hope and encouragement for the future. Every day that went by without a new liver for Michelle was a loss. Children with this condition rarely lived to age three, and Michelle was almost two.

Our mission was gaining momentum, but our fundraising up to that point was far from enough; still, the hope of better results kept us pushing forward. I would continually remind myself of the old Chinese proverb, "A journey of a thousand miles begins with a single step." I had first heard that saying as a child; it gave me hope then and now.

I learned that, in order for large organizations to make a significant donation, we had to make things official. We set up Angels, Inc. as a nonprofit with the mission of saving children's lives, beginning with Michelle, and then others. Suddenly, companies and wealthy philanthropists who had previously said no were now able to donate, but the greatest overall donations came in a dollar at a time from ordinary people just like me, who lived paycheck to paycheck. The public's heart was as touched by Michelle as mine had been. It felt good that I wasn't the only person who responded so strongly, and my confidence grew, enabling me to work even more aggressively.

People contacted me from all over the country to learn more about Michelle's condition. While I welcomed everybody who came forward and formed teams and committees of volunteers, one gentleman stood out in my mind.

Mr. Raymond Cioffi was a Vietnam vet and brilliant businessman. He was also a member of the Kiwanis Club of nearby Hurstbourne, and during our campaign, he became president of their organization. Ray was a hair client of mine who learned firsthand about the work we were doing while he sat in my stylist chair, as so many customers had before him.

Ray worked tirelessly through Kiwanis to help Michelle's cause. He eventually invited me to speak at one of their Kiwanis meetings. I appreciated his interest and felt honored to be invited to talk to these people who had done so much for the community. After my speech, the group immediately set out to help alleviate the Schmitt family's financial hardship, working hand in hand with Angels, Inc.

The club first set up a raffle and raised $2,400. The group presented a check to the family at a dinner held in their honor. By this time,

Michelle had been hospitalized due to the most recent complication brought on by her condition, her grandmother Barbara at her side. I introduced Ed and Ashley, and then Ed thanked the group and explained the difficulties of Michelle's condition and this latest setback. You could see tears in the eyes of some members, especially those with young children, and they redoubled their efforts.

Over the next two years, the Hurstbourne Kiwanis club hosted several fundraising events and enlisted the help of local and national clubs in our mission.

The Angels, Inc. fundraising efforts were doing very well, but the money was not nearly enough. Medication costs absorbed the money as fast as we made it, and other bills kept piling up. We had grown from one person to an entire community of individuals and groups, but we needed more help—perhaps a big event of some kind.

As we worked, Ed continued working as many hours as he could to support his family. Michelle struggled more and more while they waited for that all-important phone call.

In some ways, fundraising began to take on a life of its own. People came forward in overwhelming ways to help us on our mission to save Michelle's life, each one doing their part, becoming members of our growing network of angels. We had no idea we were going to need so much help.

This experience again brought me back to my teen years. I knew that I couldn't survive my home situation, but neither could I extricate myself from it on my own. I needed help also, and lots of it; then my own angels of mercy appeared.

12

Rebel's Regret

SEPTEMBER 1961

As I finished junior high school, the atmosphere in my home seemed to grow worse day by day. My mother's drinking and her mental state seemed to worsen, and the tension bubbled over more and more frequently. My situation had become critical. I had to take that first step. No one else could do it for me.

I would suffer greatly, feeling torn between what was right for me and what would keep my parents happy. In spite of everything, I loved them. I hoped that with time, we all could be happy again, after we put some emotional distance between us. I desperately wanted my parents to accept me, love me, approve of me, to see who I really was, but if I expressed anything deep and personal, they would ridicule me and say I was getting "too big for my britches."

My decision, to others, probably seems like a simple and relatively small act of teenage rebellion, but for me it was a huge step with much bigger consequences than one of my friends might suffer from their parents. It all started with an invitation.

I often received invites from my girlfriends to sleepovers on weekends, sock hops at school, and sports events. I felt forced to give excuses like illness or being too busy. I wanted to join this group of girls, who were all from nice, ordinary families. I was vulnerable and needy, and their kind offers stirred a hopefulness in me.

My first act of rebellion was to slip away from home to attend a sleepover at a friend's house with eight other girls from school.

It sounded exciting to while away the night with friends, talking about boys, eating snacks, and playing records.

I was fifteen years old at the time and finally stepping out into the world on my own without asking for permission. Although I was determined to go, I still worried about my parents. I didn't want to cause them any undue anxiety, but I doubted they would call the police to report me as missing.

That Friday after school, I returned home to change my clothes and hid my pajamas in my purse. The weather was pleasant, and the walk to Mary Jo's house wasn't very long. I was looking forward to a sleepover, only having heard how much fun they were. Having simple fun, so ordinary for those girls, would be a new experience for me.

At home I took a deep breath and walked out the front door while my mother busied herself in the back of the house. I walked down the street, just as big as you please, toward my destination. The sun was setting behind the treetops, glaring in my face and energizing me in my dash to freedom.

As I walked on, many thoughts crossed my determined mind, both positive and negative, as I debated whether I had made the right decision. I kept telling myself I had no other choice if I wanted to experience anything different from my parents' carousing lifestyle.

This was a hard step. I had always prided myself on doing the right thing, but as I turned the corner to Mary Jo's block I reminded myself of all that had pushed me to this point.

Walking faster, as if to outpace my demons, I finally arrived at my friend's house. I walked up to the door and rang the bell. I was immediately greeted by Mary Jo's mother, Dorothy, who welcomed me with a warm smile. I introduced myself.

"Oh, it's so nice to meet you, Sharon. Mary Jo says this is your first girlfriend sleepover. Hope you enjoy it."

I was absolutely tongue-tied and just nodded my head repeatedly. As I walked into their house, I imagined how nice it would be to have a mother who graciously welcomed my friends to our house instead of shooing them away.

In the kitchen was a table filled with cookies, cakes, and glasses of milk. I just stood back, astonished by this offering.

Dorothy put a hand on my shoulder. "It's all right, dear. Go help yourself." I was almost brought to tears by this woman's warmth and generosity. I just wasn't used to anybody treating me like that.

Mary Jo handed me a glass of milk. "Try the shortbread cookies first; they're delicious."

This welcome pretty much settled the issue of whether I had made the right decision or not. I was like a wanderer stranded in the desert who finally comes upon an oasis. While I drank my milk and ate a cookie, I also inhaled the emotional ambiance of the moment.

When the first group of girls arrived, they were surprised and excited to see me. Shrill screams of girlish delight filled the kitchen as they rushed over and practically knocked me over. I had to put down my milk to absorb an endless round of hugs and kisses. Years of loneliness seemed to evaporate in minutes.

After we all settled down, I had a brief moment of sadness, pondering all the years I had been deprived of their warm company. I had to wonder if my parents realized the misery they caused me through the years or if they even cared about anything other than their next drink.

That night, I had the time of my life working on puzzles, playing charades, dancing to The Beatles and Rolling Stones songs. We played a game where we shared our most embarrassing moments in life. I won hands down, sharing my story of waking up in another drunken couple's car one morning. I can't imagine how shocking that revelation must have been to them; to me, it was just one of so many embarrassing moments I had experienced. I didn't even come close in the funniest moment contest, as I had almost no funny memories in my past.

Dorothy stayed up with us, plying us with drinks and snacks half the night. She even let her hair down, as they say, and danced along with us at one point. I just stared at her in disbelief. Then, finally, she put us all to bed with kind but firm words. *Is this how 'real' mothers act?* I wondered.

The next morning I awoke to the smiling faces of giddy girls in curlers, running through the house and gathering up their stray belongings. We ate breakfast with Dorothy and her husband, Jim, who was dressed in Bermuda shorts and a knit shirt, ready for a round of golf with his buddies. *So this is what it's like to live the life of a normal fifteen-year-old teenage girl,* I thought.

As I walked home that morning, the sun shining in my face, I felt bolstered by this experience and craved more of it. I was unsure of what my reception at home would be, but concluded that this adventure was well worth it.

This overnight visit showed me what real family life could be. The open and tolerant atmosphere guided by a firm hand was refreshing. This was quite the opposite of what I grew up with, unable to express my feelings, only allowed to follow my parents' dictates.

But like caged animals that are afraid to leave when the doors are flung open, I felt my conditioning reassert itself with each homeward step. Walking away from home now seemed easier than going back. I wondered what my punishment would be, but I was anxious to face the consequences and get it over with.

When I finally arrived home, I was surprised to find that my parents were gone. They had not left a note alerting me to where they were, but then, I didn't leave one either. I sat on the swing under a large tree in the front yard, passing the time.

For the first hour, I thought about my father, whom I adored. Throughout my many trials and tribulations with my mother, I had never encountered any problems with my father. He was a kind and simple man, with a dry sense of humor, and the last person I'd ever want to hurt. I feared that my night away might have damaged our unique relationship. Of course, in my eyes, my father was not responsible for how my mother treated me. In reality, he was just as responsible, as every father is. He was certainly responsible for dragging me along on their drinking binges when I was a young child. As a teen, any hope I had of protection from my mother would be through my father.

Then my thoughts moved on to my mother, wondering how she had reacted to my rebellion. I now know she had a troubled youth, which may have caused her severe reaction to my teenage years. Later I would learn a few revelations about her life and come to empathize with her.

I remembered when I was very young, I came home from school and found her weeping like a defenseless child. I had never seen her vulnerable in any way and never would again. Remembering that moment softened my anger toward her. She was a young, innocent girl like me once. What had happened to her?

After my third hour of waiting, my concern for them took over. I recalled how careless my parents were when they drank heavily, the accidents and dangerous things that happened. Driving drunk would be a big problem, but even worse, they might have gotten stranded on their boat.

The garage where they kept the boat was always locked and didn't have any windows. While I could drive their car when they were drunk, I had never operated the boat. I remembered being out with them once; Dad sped around the lake until he hit a log, and we had to be towed to shore.

About five o'clock that Saturday evening, they returned, towing their boat behind them. Nothing was said about my disappearance, but the enforced silence spoke louder than words. I was so glad to see them home safely that I couldn't do enough for them. I fixed dinner and cleaned up afterward as they retired early.

When I finally got to bed, I lay there and didn't think about the previous night's wonderful experience, but rather my long, unusual, and twisted day. Some might have thought my parents' reaction to my absence of simply being gone all day enjoying their boat on the water without leaving a note was either a sign of their indifference to me, a way to give me a taste of my own medicine, or a diabolical way to manipulate me and play with my emotions. I saw it as a human reaction that expressed how hurt they were; to me it was almost endearing. Years later as I reflected back, I wondered: Was this a sign of how dysfunctional our relationship had become? Or of how broken I was inside?

I decided to work harder to develop a good relationship with both of them and to ask permission for any further sleepovers and outside events. I had a feeling—really a hope—that, after this weekend, they would be more open and less restrictive in the future. I could not imagine what was to come.

• • •

LOOKING BACK, I now recalled my first visit to the Schmitt's house. Barbara wholeheartedly welcomed me, in a way that reminded me of Dorothy. Seeing Ashley and Michelle looking on from behind their grandmother's skirt reminded me that they, too, like me that long-ago day, were in desperate need of the kindness of others, of more help, from more people, than they could ever dream.

13

The Game

OCTOBER 1961

After so many negative things had happened to me so early in life, this sleepover respite helped me rally my resolve to improve the direction my life was headed. I realized that changing my attitude toward my parents might help. At least it was worth a try.

I thought the first step would be to earn my privileges from that point on. Even though I already had a lot of responsibilities around the house, I resolved to help even more with my mother's housework and to work in the yard with Dad. Instead of showing me any positive feedback, my parents took advantage of my new repentant attitude by assigning more and more tasks.

I could not see that my new situation went far above and beyond the normal responsibilities children might be expected to have at home. While I was working so hard under the assumption that I was earning future privileges, I was also desperately seeking their approval and love. They had me completely under their psychological control, something that experts now easily identify as classic dysfunctional behavior for alcoholics and those in their family.

The household tasks I was assigned were never-ending, but I applied myself and tackled them head-on with a willingness that surprised even me, all the while keeping up excellent grades in school. I hoped with all of my heart that they would appreciate my efforts and give back a little of themselves as well. They didn't.

While they did acknowledge the effort I put forth, in the end, it only led to a heartbreaking situation. I finally began to realize, again, that I was not in any way to blame—that *I* was not the problem.

I had to accept who my parents were and that they would not change. I would just have to find my own way to break away from them. This escape happened with the help of some very special, caring people, more of my ordinary angels, who understood my situation and were willing to help.

This event was the turning point of my adolescence. The worst was yet to come in my life, but my overall goal as I approached my sixteenth birthday was to improve my present circumstances. As horrid as it was, this incident was a final breakthrough to a new beginning for all of us.

By now, I was a freshman in high school, settling in as the first few weeks of the year sped past. Soon it was time for spirit week, the buildup to our school's homecoming football game. This was the event of the year that everyone anxiously awaited, which would be followed by a sock hop and a bonfire. Saturday's dance would feature the crowning of the homecoming queen for the following year.

Almost every student in the school attended these glorious events. This game would decide the county football championship, which revved up our excitement. Every hallway and classroom had posters, banners, and pom-poms. We all had confetti in our hair by the end of each day as our spirits built up.

I waited until the middle of the week to ask permission from my parents to attend this great event. The home atmosphere had been better than usual. Despite her continued drinking, my mother even joked that she was now a lady of leisure, given all my help around the house.

Wednesday night's dinner was served at six o'clock sharp, and I had set the table nicely. I helped my mother with the cooking, although I was not a very good cook. I arranged the ingredients for her and cleaned up the mess afterward.

Dad seemed pleased with the friendly overtures between my mother and me as we sat down to our meal. After dinner we all shared stories about our busy day. Then, when it came to my turn,

I told them about the homecoming game and the festivities, and asked their permission to attend.

A brief silence followed my simple request. Then my father looked at me and said in a solemn tone, "We'll see."

This was not a no, so I was encouraged. I was then advised that it depended on my performance for the rest of the week, but I had no problem with that. I continued contributing as I had over the past few weeks.

The remainder of the week went well; I even washed my father's car and fed the dogs. I dusted and vacuumed the house until it was sparkling clean. And then I patiently waited for Friday night.

The big day I had been waiting for finally came. The school was at a fever pitch with the big game at stake and everyone wondering who would be crowned homecoming queen. The anxiety was exhausting but also very exciting.

I assumed that my request would be granted to attend the event; my work had been flawless, my attitude pleasant, not a single misstep. They had no reason to deny my request; I had done everything they required and more. I dressed that day in blue and gold, our school colors. School was so much fun that day. The excitement was tangible as we anticipated the events of that evening.

On the way to school, the boys passing by in their cars had blue and gold streamers flowing in the wind. They were honking their horns and cheering us all on to a rousing victory. I couldn't help but get excited by the promise this night held.

Toward the end of the day, the school had a pep rally in the gymnasium, ratcheting up the fervor as the team's players stepped out on the stage to join in the cheers. Everyone was delirious, and some people had to sit down to catch their breath.

I was hyped up to the hilt and hurried home to prepare for the evening's events, but when I opened the door and walked into the house, you could cut the tension in the air with a knife. The shades were drawn, and the living room was dark.

Partially propped up against the wall, my mother sat there amid her beer bottles. One open bottle lingered in her shaky hand as she tried to draw it up to her mouth, hitting her cheek instead.

Her eyes were glazed over, and I could sense her vile mood from across the room. I thought it best just to leave her alone. I hurried

past her and down the hallway to my bedroom. This scene wasn't
new to me; I tried to just dismiss it.

I was determined to keep positive and continued to carry out
my week-long, prearranged plans as if everything were all right. I
started running my bathwater while I laid out my clothes, threw
some curlers in my long, curly hair, and took a bath.

Afterward, I immediately went back to my room to dress and
comb my hair for the evening, rushing so I could get out of the
house while my mother was still dazed. I hoped I could sneak out
and avoid the usual scathing attacks I received when she was this
drunk.

As I put on my pink lipstick for the finishing touch, I turned to
hurry out the bedroom door. But my mother stood in the hallway,
leaning against the wall and blocking my way. Her arms folded,
she scowled at me, as angry as I had ever seen her.

"Where in the hell do you think you're going?"

Stunned by her aggressive stance, I feebly replied, "To the football game as we talked about."

"Like [****], you are." She then staggered over, grabbed me by
the hair, and pulled me into the bathroom. Mom took a wet towel
and started to rub my makeup and lipstick off, scraping her long
fingernails across my face with every rough pass.

Her breath reeked with the smell of beer as she screamed, "With
that pink lipstick, you look like a teenage tramp, just like your
mother did! And I'm going to teach you a lesson, right here and
now, you little tramp!"

I was powerless against her vicious attack, my body tossed
around like a rag doll. I tried to break free, but she had a firm hold
on my hair. I looked around the room for a hairbrush to fight back
but didn't see one.

Her coarse, slurred words screamed in my ear: "You have bad
genes, and don't you forget it, Missy. You don't have me fooled for
one minute, you little tramp. But I'm going to straighten you out
but good!"

I was shocked, both by her physical attack and by what she was
saying to me. After spending time with my birth mother, Anna,
after all of the other abusive things she had said and done to me
over the past three years, I still thought we had gotten past her

insane paranoia over my chastity. My mind was spinning. What could I say or do to get out of this? Frightened, I struggled to break free, but she outweighed me by fifty pounds.

Finally, I pulled away from her strong grasp, but she grabbed my father's large leather belt from his clothes hanging on the back of the bathroom door. Mom whipped me across the back, and then struck my face with it, breaking the skin and leaving marks.

I pushed past her out into the hall, and she chased me from room to room, swinging the belt at me and leaving welts all over my body, back and front. Finally, I reached the front door, flung it open, and raced out into the street. She didn't follow me.

I broke down in tears, which mixed with the blood from her fingernail scrapes across my face, swollen from the many welts beginning to rise up. The sleeves of my pretty dress were torn to shreds. My mother had just beaten me in a drunken rage. I had been hit before, whipped with a belt before, but this time was the worst yet. Tonight, there would be no football game, no dance. I had to figure out what to do.

As I sobbed profusely, I tried to straighten my hair and fix my appearance. Finally, a kind neighbor who had apparently over-heard our fight and saw me rush out of the house, bleeding, crying, my clothes in tatters, came over. She took me to the safety of her home and begged me not to return until my father came home.

She was aware of my mother's drinking problem and went on to say that everyone in the neighborhood knew about it. This revela-tion was the first time I had ever heard that from another person. I wondered if she knew about the other beatings.

My deep, hidden secret for all of those years was not solely mine after all. This should have been a relief, but the shame and embarrassment I felt only made it worse. *But, if everyone knew, why hadn't people come forward or told the police?* I wondered to myself, trying to sort through everything.

My father soon returned from work to what he thought would be a settled home atmosphere. As he pulled his car into the garage, I crossed the street and met him as he stepped out of his car.

As he looked up to me to greet me with a warm smile, he focused on my injuries and torn dress. His concern was obvious. "Sharon, what happened to you?"

As I puckered up, trying not to cry, my lower lip began to quiver as I said, "Mom did this to me."

He looked confused. "Honey, what did you do to provoke her?" Of course, his first assumption was that I was to blame.

As tears rolled down my face, I replied, "Nothing."

He said, "You must have done something wrong."

I realized in that instant that my mother was flawless in his eyes, and he had no idea how sick she really was. I said, "I was just getting ready to go to the game. That's all."

He still looked confused. I stepped into the house, avoiding my mother, and put my pajamas in my purse again. I was determined to get away from both of them. I left to find peace somewhere else.

14

Exodus

OCTOBER 1961–JUNE 1962

This rapid exodus was unplanned, and I was already exhausted and physically hurt by my confrontation with my mother. My emotional state was shattered far worse than the wounds the beating inflicted on me. I was confused, crushed, and exposed, with nowhere to go.

I started walking with no direction in mind, and soon found myself across the street in the woods. I sat down on a big tree stump, trying to come to grips with my devastating disappointment. Dark thoughts swirled around inside my mind.

All of my confusion and emotional pain finally got the best of me, and I broke down and cried my heart out in the woods. I felt totally alone in the world and abandoned by my family—again. My classmates were having the time of their lives at the game. I was sure no one was looking for me, no one was worried about me, or even realized I was missing. No one.

I was scared to death, but it was getting dark, and I had to think of somewhere to go for the night. I pulled myself together and stopped crying, and my mind drifted to my biological mother, Anna. *No*, I immediately decided. Her family had pushed me away and would not welcome me back, even for a night, even though I was badly beaten.

I calmed myself down and headed out of the woods toward my girlfriend's house, where I had attended the slumber party. When Dorothy opened the door and saw me, she quickly brought me inside. She ran hot water for a bath in the tub and let me soak while she cleaned my welts and cuts.

Afterward, Dorothy got one of her daughter's dresses, and I changed into it. Mary Jo wouldn't be home from the game and dance for some time. I sat with her mother and told her about Mom's drinking problem and what led to this beating.

I was afraid to overstate the situation. I remembered that Anna could not, or would not, believe me when I told her about my mother. Why should anyone else? I tried to brush it off, adding, "Mom gets this way when she's drunk, and this isn't the first time she's called me a tramp."

"Sharon, there's no excuse for her behavior. You're a lovely teenage girl just dressing up for a big school event."

I did not tell her any more about my history, about my childhood, about my birth mother, Anna, and the confrontation that had led to Mom telling me I was adopted. It was bad enough learning that everybody in the neighborhood knew about my alcoholic parents.

Mary Jo arrived home to find me sitting in her living room with welts and bruises on my face and arms. She immediately sat next to me and held my hand as I told her about what had happened.

She looked to her mother, who nodded her head. "You're staying with us for a couple of days until we can get to the bottom of this."

I broke out in tears and gave Mary Jo a big hug. Dorothy asked if I had eaten dinner yet, and I confessed that I hadn't. She fixed me a chicken potpie while Mary Jo and I sat in the game room and watched TV. That night I slept in Mary Jo's big bed.

I stayed with Mary Jo's family over the weekend, but I had to return home Sunday night to prepare for school the following day. I had no choice in the matter. This time my walk home was different. I would suffer through any consequences, but I didn't really care about their reaction one way or the other.

As I entered the house, the atmosphere was cold and uninviting. I walked past my mother, looking straight ahead. She sarcastically asked, "Well, did you find someone to feel sorry for you?"

I shuddered at the sheer nerve of the woman, but I turned and looked her in the eyes. "Yes," I answered defiantly. "There are still some decent people around here."

She only snickered in return, but I no longer feared her, and I now had some kind and sympathetic people where I could seek refuge if this ever happened again. I went to my room and dressed for bed several hours early. I stayed there, spending the time thinking about my situation.

I made a vow to myself while lying in bed that night: if I ever had a child, I would honor and respect them as individual human beings. I promised myself I would never allow myself to become a slave to alcohol as my mother was.

The following Monday was a typical day at school, until my third-period gym class. After playing volleyball, we had to take showers to get a full grade. Just like all of the other girls, I undressed, entered the shower, and filed past our teacher, Miss Clevenger, to get checked off. After my shower, Miss Clevenger firmly told me, "Sharon, I want to see you in my office right away."

I had no idea what I had done wrong to get called to her office, but I quickly got dressed and met her outside the locker room.

Without explanation, she said, "Follow me."

While trying to keep up with her quick pace, I could tell that she was very angry and upset. I didn't say a word, not wanting to aggravate her further.

We arrived shortly at the girls' counselor's office, but it was empty. Miss Clevenger told me, "Sit down, Sharon, and don't move until I get back."

I just sat there and wondered what I could have done wrong. Nothing unusual happened during the volleyball class. My mind kept spinning, trying to figure out why I was there.

I really liked our gym teacher; she had been on the volleyball team in college and taught us a lot of plays and techniques. I hoped I had not disappointed her in any way, but after Friday's events and Sunday night's cold reception at home, I really didn't need anybody, even this kind teacher, singling me out, or worse, notifying my parents of something I had unknowingly done.

Suddenly the door flew open, and my teacher and both of the girls' deans stepped into the room. Again, my first thought was that I must have done something awful for her to summon both of them.

Miss Clevenger told me abruptly and without explanation, "Sharon, take off your outer clothes, please."

I was reluctant and humiliated, as this would expose the extent of Mom's beating. I obeyed her and disrobed down to my underwear. They stepped closer and walked around me, noting the bruises, cuts, and scrapes on my battered body.

One of the deans, a woman in her forties, softly asked me, "Sharon, who did this to you?"

I shook my head. "Please, let's just drop it. It'll only make matters worse."

She asked pointedly, "Sharon, did your parents do this to you?"

I looked down at the floor as tears rolled down my cheeks. "I beg you to please leave it alone. Mom was drunk, and she gets mean when she drinks too much."

"I'm sorry, Sharon. But for your safety, we must make sure this never happens again." She reached over and put her arms around me for reassurance, but nothing she or any of them could do or say would relieve my fears.

I understood their mandate as schoolteachers, and I could respect, even appreciate, their concern, but I was fearful of the consequences at home.

When she said that they were going to call my parents in for a meeting, I begged them not to bother them. In particular, I told them Dad couldn't leave work without its own consequences.

Miss Clevenger now took a sheet of paper and wrote down the size and position of every mark on me. Afterward, the women all signed and dated the report as witnesses, and I was allowed to put my clothes back on.

While they were dead serious about preventing further abuse, I knew calling in my parents and accusing them of beating me would make my mother furious. And I worried my father would be upset, having been called off the job. It never occurred to me that my father might be more upset about the beating than his work.

They moved me to another office, and I remained there until my parents arrived. I watched them pass down the hall through the office windows; my mother was again in a drunken stupor. She seemed to snicker at me as she passed by.

I sat there for forty minutes while they talked; I couldn't imagine the conversation they were having, and my parents' reaction to it. Yet, I was more concerned about what would happen next, frightened of going home with them in Dad's car. What would they do to me?

When the door to the office finally opened, my father stepped out and was as angry as I had ever seen him. His facial expression was stern, and his teeth clenched tight.

Miss Clevenger retrieved me from the office. She could apparently see my fear. "It's all right, Sharon. Your parents understand. This won't happen again."

My father just looked at me and commanded, "Let's go."

I sat in the back seat of the car, looking out the window at the three women standing there, waving goodbye to me. My gym teacher kept waving as our car pulled away. I knew she was on my side, like Mary Jo's mother; maybe everything would be all right after all.

Not a word was spoken on the drive home, but I could see that both my parents were furious. Before, I only had one angry parent, but now I had two. When we arrived home, I was surprised by my father.

"Sharon, go to your room. I need to talk with your mother."

This was encouraging. Did Dad finally realize how sick Mom was? Would he finally do something about it? I could only hope. Later, he brought me a plate of chicken and rice for dinner but still wasn't finished talking with Mom. He told me to eat my dinner and go to bed.

I ate the food and placed the dinner plate outside my door. Then, I lay in bed and wondered what was happening in the dining room. Whatever the resolution, it couldn't be any worse than it already was.

Miss Clevenger was very kind to me at school the next day, asking me if things went all right at home. I told her my parents had a long talk, and they both seemed better in the morning. But, by school mandate, she checked every day to see if there were signs of any further abuse.

My teacher and counselors had become three more angels in my life. But, ultimately, my mother's physical threats worsened, once attempting to burn my face with a hot iron. Instead of cowering, I started defending myself. I was strong, and afraid one day I might actually hurt my mother, I responded by staying away from home as much as possible. When the situation was dangerous, I was emboldened to run away, which I did, over and over. I developed a network of friends whose parents would take me in for a night or two, and that is how I spent the remainder of my life at home.

• • •

BACK IN THE present, more angels of mercy appeared to help with our fundraising campaign for Ashley and Michelle. And they came just in time.

15

Ordinary Angels

1993

I made a new friend who was willing to help with our fundraising campaign. Millie Sola was the owner of *Entertainer Magazine* and a recent hair client. She was a spirited, fun-loving Puerto Rican spitfire who joined me to raise money for Michelle's surgery, transportation, and medications.

Millie had no idea that I was the president of Angels, Inc. She had seen the posters around town for the hair-a-thon but had been too busy to participate. I told her what we were doing for the Schmitt family and that I was overwhelmed between work, fundraising activities, and keeping in touch with the Schmitt family.

Millie asked more questions about our fundraising efforts. Then I went on to explain about the organization and our mission to help Michelle get a new liver.

"I take it that's not chopped liver!" she teased, lightening the mood.

I needed a good laugh by now. I went on to explain the intricate circumstances surrounding Michelle's transplant. Millie immediately understood the urgency of this situation, and she joined in wholeheartedly to help our efforts.

The two of us were like Felix and Oscar in *The Odd Couple*, as opposite as night and day, but we shared the same concern for the girls. I traded public relations services in exchange for advertising our events and writing up stories about the Schmitt family's troubles in her magazine.

Millie was very talented, and the two of us complemented each other very well, developing ideas for stories and fundraising events. Like me, Millie had her own childhood troubles and could relate to Michelle's desperate needs. Millie's compassion came through in her stories and drew a great response from her readers.

The people of Louisville had really embraced our mission. I would be fixing somebody's hair a few feet away from the front door, and little kids would come in and ask about the girls. Families and youth groups would hold bake sales, and mothers would drop off the money they raised. Others would just open the door and hand me donations.

One day, a group of kids appeared at the salon and handed me a bag of money. The little curly-haired leader said, "This is for Michelle and Ashley." I was on my break at the time, and I opened the bag, expecting a pile of coins and dollar bills. The total came to nearly $900.

I stooped over and told them, "Thank you. The girls appreciate your help very much." I gave the little girl a big hug. I watched them walk to the corner where two of the mothers waited for them. I didn't have a name, so I logged the donation in as "The Little Angels Bake Sale."

This would happen quite often, but usually not as large of a donation. One time I interrupted a dye job on a client to receive a donation another children's group was dropping off. When I turned back to my client, she had tears running down her face.

"My goodness, Sharon, what you're doing is amazing. Those kids are learning a life lesson about the value of helping others."

All of these precious angels taking it upon themselves to do something for Michelle allowed me to see how this mission had focused our community on the higher divine purpose we all have of helping those in need. I was sure that our tireless efforts would come back to our community, and to us, tenfold.

Another time I was walking past a ValuMarket grocery store when the store manager chased me down and handed me a check for the girls. He told me how much he appreciated what I was doing and wished he could do more. I told him every little bit helped. The check was for $100.

As the fundraising effort expanded, I often felt inadequate and unprepared, but there were lots of things I knew how to do and did well. I wrote letters to local businesses night after night and then to politicians, judges, and lawyers. Some large personal donations came from that outreach, as well as a few corporate funds.

As I mentioned earlier, I also made personal visits and many phone calls. My first calls were to airlines and companies with private jets who could fly Michelle to Omaha to get her liver transplant, but their help didn't stop there.

One of my clients was Rick Laughlin, who was in management at KFC Corporation. I had cut his hair for years and never knew what he did for the company. Then, out of the blue, he asked how the girls were doing. I told him that the call for Michelle's transplant could happen soon, but we would only have a six-hour window to get her in the air and on the way once we got the call.

I told him I had lined up several airlines for the flight, but given their busy schedules, I might need a corporate jet. Rick's eyes lit up as he told me that he was responsible for scheduling KFC's executive jet. If their jet was available when the call came, they'd fly Michelle to Omaha. I added KFC to my list.

Pattco was another early respondent to my jet team call. I had never met their president, Jim Patterson, but both Jim and one of his pilots, Jason, took an extra interest in our mission. They wanted to be the ones to fly her out. They had one request: a picture of the girls to hang in the plane hangar.

I recalled a quote on the Hair Angels' T-shirts we wore at the original hair-a-thon: "With God, all things are possible," a passage I continue to live by today.

One day I received a letter and a donation that stuck out more than any other. It was sent to my home address. The scratchy lettering on the envelope was hard to read. It said: "I am old and very poor, and a black woman, but I want to do something for this little girl."

There was no name or return address on this envelope, which contained a single dollar bill. I wondered if she was one of my neighbors. The letter brought tears to my eyes. She was one person I would have gone out of my way to give a special thank you, as she was compelled to share with me her race. It reminded me that a child is a child and that no matter our nationality, race, age, or financial status, we are all the same in God's eyes. Our universal love for our children unites us.

I must say that creating a nonprofit was a great business decision for the Angels. In addition to making it easier for corporations to donate money, it allowed us to work better with other nonprofits. Our mission seemed to reach a lot of them: Ronald McDonald House, Kiwanis, and others all worked with us.

Angels, Inc. always wanted purity in our message and a high-minded mission, but there were challenges along the way. Individuals, churches, private groups, companies, and other organizations took it upon themselves to organize fundraisers for us, which was tremendous, but they often had no oversight or accountability, and record-keeping became more and more challenging for us. As the effort grew around our area and the rest of the country, we were concerned that one mistake or feud could ruin our reputation and, ultimately, hurt the Schmitt family.

Certainly there were lots of other worthy causes and people asking for donations for them at the same time as Angels, Inc. One organization was upset that some annual pledges and donations were diverted to our campaign for the girls, and they left a nasty message on our voicemail. A few people used our name to throw events and pocket the money, but we believe and hope that this was very rare.

We had good results from the big glass jars we placed at drug stores, gas stations, and grocery store checkouts. Each jar featured the girls' picture, which helped. Since our campaign got nationwide attention, some chain stores asked for jars for their other locations.

I enjoyed picking up the loose change from these jars and made the rounds every week. Money collected outside the city was funneled through those stores' corporate offices, and we received regular checks from them. In addition, all the local news stations followed our campaign and gave updates on the girls, with scroll lines on where to send money.

God put a mission in front of me and nudged untold numbers of others to join the cause. Its energy was contagious. This campaign's appeal cut across all boundaries and unified Louisville and the entire state like no other cause, with thousands of regular people each giving just a little of their hard-earned money to help. The donations kept accumulating, whether it was through spare pocket change, $1,000 checks, or a poor woman's last dollar. Every penny was someone's sacrifice, and we took those sacrifices seriously.

The caring spirit aroused by this kind of selfless endeavor affects everyone. This outpouring reminded me of how my own rescue by neighbors and teachers changed my parents and set straight the course of my youth. Never doubt the power of the smallest act of kindness, the slightest effort to get involved when God nudges your heart.

16

Reprieve

1962–1964

For the rest of my time in high school, my relationship with my parents remained cool but cordial. I would not then, nor ever, receive the parental affection and wisdom from them that I longed for and needed, but many years later we did find our way closer to a new, healthier, "normal" adult relationship.

Looking back, had I enjoyed a strong and healthy family life, I wonder if learning about Ashley and Michelle Schmitt would have pricked my heart so deeply, or if I would have been as willing to sacrifice so much to help them. I cannot say that I wouldn't change everything I went through given the chance, but I do know that what the Bible says in Romans 8:28 is true: God does use everything we experience for our good, for those of us who are called according to his purposes. He may have allowed my experiences to prepare me for a tremendous challenge many years in the future, but as a teenage girl on the brink of womanhood, I had no idea what was up ahead. I was just trying to get through high school, keep myself on a healthy path, but also make up for my lost youth as best as I could.

My gym teacher, Miss Clevenger, got me involved in several different school sports activities. As a young child I had taken gymnastics lessons at the American Turners club, an organization focused on physical education that is still active today. This worked out well for my parents, as the club had a bar where they could drink while I had my lessons. Still, this training stuck with me and helped me fit in nicely with her gymnastics program. As a result, I spent a lot of after-school hours there, which kept me safely away from home.

She also got me involved in the school's track and field program. That year I broke a record in my weight class for running the 1500-meter event, which required running around the football field almost four times. I took my first small trophy home and put it on my bedroom dresser.

I never told my parents about these activities and was very careful not to flaunt my new achievements, afraid of any disruption in my routine. But I could see the difference in my own attitude and energy level as I became more physically fit. I had found what I was looking for: a healthy, positive outlet and new adult mentors to guide my life.

The first change I saw in my mother's attitude toward me was when she found the track trophy in my room. She placed it on the television set in the living room. That day, I came home from school to find my mother showing the trophy to some of our neighbors. She bragged about how proud she was of me, and even kissed me on the cheek. My mother's delight seemed genuine, as if the previous year's school summons and Dad's reaction to it had finally gotten through to her.

This turnaround stunned me, and I graciously accepted their accolades. I was getting plenty of emotional support from friends and neighbors, but I really wanted my mom to be part of my new life, outside the house. While my involvement in high school had a huge impact on me, at each event I saw stands full of parents and family. I imagined what it would be like to have her there, healthy, sober, cheering me on like other parents. But she was reclusive by nature, and that would take some time. And my worst nightmare come true would be for her to show up drunk to one of my events, something that had happened to me before.

I eventually invited her to a gymnastics meet one Saturday afternoon. Catching her off guard that morning, I said, "Mom, I want you to go with me to my meet this afternoon."

She appeared surprised. "Are you sure?"

I knew she felt, given our tattered history, that I was ashamed of her. This invitation was a chance for me to show her that all was forgiven. By this time, Mom never went anywhere outside of the house; this would be a challenge for her.

"Yes, I'm sure," I replied. "This is a difficult meet, and I need your support out there." I hugged her.

She was so funny rushing around and getting ready for the outing, beaming over my simple invitation. I could see that she was as starved for my attention now as I had been my entire childhood and youth, and I determined I would make an effort to include Mom more in my life. Hopefully, this would open her up to other healthy social activities, something she had not experienced in many years.

Inside the school gymnasium, I sat her on the bottom row of the bleachers so she would have a clear view of the events. When I did well in one of my routines, she would clap her hands, telling anyone who would listen, "That's my daughter over there."

I don't know if it was her presence cheering me on, but I had one of my best gymnastic performances that day. After each routine, I could hear her telling everyone, "My daughter's the best."

That event along with other sports meets my mother would later attend were precious memories. And at the time, it showed me how my mother and I both needed each other. I had not yet learned what happened to her as a child, but I wondered if her parents, who had passed away long ago, were ever affectionate with her.

That day watching us from the coach's box was my gym teacher. She had taken the first bold steps to stop my abuse and to confront my parents, which changed everything for them and for me. And her influence extended far beyond my athletic school career.

Miss Clevenger was my most ardent mentor and supporter. She taught me how to stay fiercely focused in sports, not letting anything distract me from my performance goal. She also helped me forgive my parents and eventually forgive myself as well, letting go of the burdens I had been carrying all those years. After high school, we would stay in touch for years.

The time invested by these caring people changed my world. Another person who stands out was a neighbor who took me to church twice a week. Dorothy, Mary Jo's mom, was a firm believer in God and stepped up to protect me when I needed it the most. She stayed with me, including me in her family's church activities through the rest of my high school years, and this experience became a foundation for my own faith. Dorothy and her daughter remained at my side for many years.

On the weekends, when I wasn't involved with sports, Dorothy came to my home to pick me up for sleepovers at their house. She passed no judgment on my parents, treating them very cordially. But, she set herself as an example for my parents on how to conduct themselves. These people—teachers, counselors, parents, neighbors, coaches—saved my life. They were most definitely angels on earth for me.

As time went on, it felt as if my peers went out of their way to include me. My popularity soared, and the invites to sleepovers and other teenage activities increased.

Then came the best honor of all—for me, at least. The Durrett Boosters Club held a dance one Friday night, during which they would crown a king and queen, based on "penny-a-vote" solicitations collected from classmates. This annual event raised funds for school improvements and a scholarship. After weeks of pennies being collected in voting boxes, the results were in, and I was notified I would be crowned queen! My selection was such a boost for me. Since I had done my best to keep my woes to myself, perhaps word of my situation had gotten out and struck a chord with my fellow students. Together with Warner Anderson as king, I was given a trophy, some beautiful flowers, and we were featured in the *Jefferson Report* paper.

I borrowed a beautiful white dress to wear for the occasion, with a skirt billowing with white tulle, and white high heels. It was a magical night for me, such a turnaround from my horrible homecoming trauma not that long before. The next day, my parents snapped a photo before I had to return the dress.

It took time to adjust to this change in my parents' attitude toward me. Of course, I was thrilled by this outpouring of respect and affection, but there also lurked the fear that Mom would regress to her abusive and drunken nature.

I had experienced how alcohol could warp one's mind. I knew deep down that Mom could be an affectionate mother from her treatment of me as a baby and young child, before her heavy drinking bouts began. I prayed that this moderation would continue.

Image courtesy of Sharon Stevens Evans.

I responded to these adjustments with love and understanding, forgiving them for their past behavior. It was tough for them to alter their lives for me, but they were also expanding outside of their old alcoholic lifestyle into something new for them.

17

Far Too Late

JULY 20, 1970

My father quit drinking shortly after the school summons, but my mother had no desire to stop, despite my father's every effort to make her quit. He loved her so much, but wouldn't take drastic measures. And, of course, you cannot force an alcoholic to stop drinking. Only they can make that choice.

He stopped taking her to the taverns. However, she always managed to buy her own beer or find a neighbor who would serve her alcohol at their house. My father was a very simple man with good values. He worked hard and stood by his word. Dad was devoted to my mother, but it was just a matter of time before her drinking would get the better of her again.

• • •

A FEW YEARS later, I was a newly single and very young mom working to support myself, and my mother cared for my young son during the day while I cut hair for a living. Looking back, I don't know how I could have thought she would behave differently with my son, more responsibly than she had when I was a child, but I had her word that she wouldn't drink while she was caring for him, and I needed help. I swore I would always treat my own children with love and take good care of them, but like many children of alcoholics, I was always willing to give her "one more chance," ultimately putting my own son at risk. I was desperate to believe her, give her a way to redeem herself—and in complete honesty, I thought he would be safer there than in a stranger's home.

They say the definition of insanity is doing something the same way over and over but expecting a different result. By this time, my father had given up drinking, and I thought my mother had as well, but she still struggled with alcohol, and eventually Derek paid the price for my decision. Thankfully, he survived that period unscathed.

This is where my history began in this journey, with my memory of Derek hiding under the yellow plastic pool. Not long into that period, my mother began to have symptoms of a failing liver, a common consequence of alcoholism, and soon after was diagnosed with liver cancer.

As Mom's illness progressed, she was hospitalized. It would not be long before alcoholism would take her life; she spent twenty-eight days in the hospital before she passed. I rarely left her side during this time. We had many long talks during those last days; she explained things I never before fully understood.

Because of her own mother's mental illness, Mom feared that she would fall victim to the same disorder one day. This obsessive fear totally destroyed her life, and indeed, her drinking may have been an attempt to mask the early signs of her own mental illness. She kept this awful secret to herself instead of getting help, only to express it when she was close to death.

The day in my childhood that I found her crying was the day she heard of her beloved mother's death. She quietly grieved her passing alone.

She apologized for her bad treatment of me and assured me that she loved me deeply. Through much of our talks, she blamed her treatment of me on her past, or on others, so her apologies were shallow in that way.

We talked about her own painful childhood and youth. I could see how her experiences may have led to her paranoia and to her own mental illness. Her experiences were horrific, but still, every-one has their own choice to make.

After all she had been through, even though she was dying as a result of her drinking, Mom still was unable to come to grips with being an alcoholic, and unable to connect her neglect and abuse as a mother to her alcoholism. She was so close to death, and we had so much between us; I decided to let her excuses slide.

She admitted after all this time that her fears about my promiscuity were unjustified, and then she told me, "Sharon, you're strong and have a good heart having to put up with so much. Use what you've learned to help others and prevent them from falling down as I did."

I replied to my dying mother, "Mom, I understood you must have had a deep secret eating away at you. I just wish you could have told someone about this, a doctor maybe, and not have had to drink away your pain."

She reached out and took my hand. "Well, we got it straight now."

Far too late, I thought, yet I assured her of how much I loved her. My memories of her when I was a child and before she started drinking were how I would choose to remember her. After that, we told each other funny stories about our time together, which seemed to dissolve any last shreds of anger or resentment.

I lost my mother one afternoon when my father came to visit her. Mom told me, "While your father's here, I want you to go home and get some rest. It's been a long day."

She reached up as I leaned over to kiss her goodbye and brushed my long hair out of my eyes. "I love you, Sharon." She murmured something about peace. There was a look in her eyes that made me hesitant to leave her, but I walked out of the room.

I left my father at her bedside, holding her hand. I was gone half an hour when she died. I was twenty-four when my mother passed away.

18

Saving Derek

1965–1971

Iresented the excruciating turmoil of my teenage years. I would have preferred that my mother had dealt with her problems and lived longer. I was torn apart by her death, but I had to go on to find my place in the world. Her last words lingered on, encouraging me to be helpful to others. Years later, they still resonated within me when confronted with Michelle and Ashley's awful situation.

Although I had never met Theresa, I felt a spiritual bond with her and her children, especially with Michelle, who was slowly dying before my eyes. These girls were innocent victims, as I had once been. Just as I had been saved by strangers who decided to step in and be my angels, I would not rest until I had paid that debt forward. I was determined to bring them back to a world of health and happiness.

We were barely raising enough money to meet the monthly medicine costs for the girls and, with Michelle's condition worsening by the day, we hopefully would soon have the expenses of the surgery and travel to cover, not to mention the ongoing medicines and complications each girl would face throughout their lives. To raise sufficient funds for our cause, I decided we would need larger events, like the musical fundraisers and national telethons held to raise money for cancer, childhood illness, and disaster relief. Putting such an event together would draw from my experience thirty years prior, gained during my first marriage, at the tender age of nineteen, to a talented musician named Wayne Young.

Wayne Young was from a good family, the oldest of six rugged boys. He was tall, handsome, with thick dark hair, deep brown eyes, a big smile, and a charismatic personality. Wayne was a college student working several jobs, a talented and successful musician who managed quite well for such a young man. We met when I was sixteen and began dating shortly after. Wayne and I discovered we were both dreamers and had a reckless devil-may-care attitude about established society and fitting into it.

Before long, our relationship became serious. By the end of my junior year in high school, I had decided to drop out of high school to attend cosmetology school. That summer I worked hard to earn enough money to pay for cosmetology school, and dropped out of high school to attend. I was ready to begin my life, excited about a fresh start. Around Christmastime 1964, I discovered I was pregnant. I found myself in the same situation my biological mother did eighteen years earlier, only Wayne and I were in love and ready to start our life together. We were married in a small ceremony in my biological mother's home. Anna and her husband were there, along with my parents, Wayne's parents, my friend, Sonya, and Wayne's friend, Tom "Cosmo" Cosdon, lead singer of Cosmo and the Counts, who Wayne was playing with at the time. Just that fast, I was out of my parents' home, newly married, and expecting our first child. Sometimes, pipe dreams have a way of actually becoming realities, and eventually one of those dreams would separate my new husband and me.

About a month after we were married, Wayne came home from work one day and said with a surge of confidence, "I quit my job this morning."

"You did?"

"Yes," he answered. "I quit school too."

I was bewildered. "Why did you do that?"

"I'm going to become a musician," he smiled. "What do you think of that?"

Most young wives would have put their foot down and said, "No! Absolutely not." But, it sounded like a great idea to me, and a whole lot of fun.

I had no idea what the world of music would be like or the consequences for our marriage down the road. I only thought of the stimulating experiences we would share, traveling across the country with Wayne's guitar and my battered suitcase, arm in arm.

For a flighty, eighteen-year-old girl who had been insulated from adventure all of her life, Wayne's proclamation was all I needed to hear. If he wanted to be a musician, then that was that. I followed alongside him through his journey to musical fame. For us as a couple, these were extraordinary and fun-filled times, even during my pregnancy.

He had assembled a great musical group called *Soul, Incorporated*. It became the hottest band in town, and they worked gigs constantly that first year. But soon, the bookings slowed down. We would have to hit the road if we were going to eat, and Wayne needed national exposure.

During the first year of our marriage, he started traveling the nightclub circuit across the country, seeking the limelight of stardom, fame, and fortune. I traveled with him most of the time and enjoyed it very much. Then he joined *Dick Clark's Caravan of Stars*, alongside the top artists in the business. It was the big break that he needed to boost him to the top.

Concert production had always interested me, and this was an excellent opportunity to observe big-time concert tours. Behind the stage, there were frantic musical directors, busy stagehands, and crews for lighting and sound scurrying all around. The pace was fast and exciting, catapulting me from stage to stage for months.

I honed my hairdressing skills on the *Caravan of Stars* road show, opening the doors for me to dress hair for celebrities such as Lou Christie, David Crosby, The Byrds, Paul Revere and the Raiders, and more. Later, I would meet Charlie Daniels, Blood Sweat and Tears, Lonnie Mack, and Roy Head. The nicest Christian performer you could ever meet was B. J. Thomas. These were good business people, working their way to the top producing and playing their music, creating some of the best pop songs of the century. I was there observing it all, and this experience would serve me well thirty years later in my efforts to help the Schmitt girls.

I never realized how having a child would affect our marriage. That summer after tour ended, I prepared as best as I could for motherhood as I entered the last three months of my pregnancy. I gave birth to my son Derek on August 6, 1965. While holding him in my arms, memories of my childhood flooded back, reminding me of the importance of a stable home life. I recalled resenting my parents and our weekends spent going from bar to bar, with me driving them home. While mesmerized by the incredible musical world we moved through, I wanted a more traditional life for my son; his needs took priority. I wanted a home to raise my child, not motels and hotels, no matter how fancy they were.

I couldn't bring myself to travel any longer, living out of a suitcase and eating restaurant food; the road was no place for a newborn. I stayed in Louisville to raise our son. My mother had some time to experience the joy of being a grandparent before she became ill and passed away. I was glad things turned out the way they did, if not just so she could have that time.

While I was very content sharing a settled life with my young son, my marriage was rapidly unraveling. My husband was into his successful music career far too deep to ever turn back. We kept up a long-distance relationship for over five years, but soon our continued separation would divide us. Heartbroken, I signed the divorce papers in March 1971.

Wayne introduced me to new worlds beyond anything I knew existed or would have ever imagined. I followed alongside him with trust, curious and eager to be part of his world of excitement and adventure. Marriage seemed like a great idea at the time. But our marriage began to fall apart before it really stood much of a chance.

When the marriage finally dissolved, it was a mutual decision, and we parted on good terms. Our friendship has remained throughout the years. Wayne kept up his relationship with his son and encouraged him in future endeavors that would bring Derek back into his father's world of musical entertainment.

It was time for me to grow up and raise my son as a good mother, but the responsibility of a newborn baby opened a whole new world for me. While I cherished the idea of motherhood, I knew nothing about babies or raising a child and could not rely on my own childhood as an example. In many ways, I was still a child myself.

Natural instinct has a way of protecting the innocent from the ignorant if one is sincere and dedicated. So for us, everything seemed to work out. I started a career as a hairdresser that put food on the table and kept a roof over our heads. I had high school friends in Louisville with families now, so Derek had many "aunts and uncles."

With Derek at my side, I stumbled along, providing for him the best way I could, although raising a child alone was daunting. When times were tough, I could look at him and see the joy he added to my life. I had someone in my life who wouldn't hurt me or leave me.

His beautiful, broad grin surrounded by thick, blond Harpo Marx curls greeted me every morning with affection. He'd curl up in my arms as close as he could get, which gave me comfort that I was not alone. As it turned out, those early years would be the best I would know for a long time to come. My adoptive parents mellowed, and we reconciled. I had hopes they had maintained sobriety "enough" to properly care for Derek while I was at work, and, for better or worse, I needed their help while he was still too young to attend school. We made it work, notwithstanding the yellow pool incident. I could not imagine that I was about to enter into the most dangerous and challenging period of my life.

19

Turning Point

1971–1991

Newly divorced and Derek in second grade, I found myself alone and vulnerable. I had never before had to provide for myself, much less an innocent child, and had to learn, with a lot of difficulty, how to manage my own affairs. After a stranger violently attacked me in my home later that first year, fear took over my whole outlook. I could not forget all I had been through in my life, nor let go of my relentless anxiety. I longed for safety and security, and just a few months later, I thought I had found it in another relationship. I remarried and changed my last name to Stevens.

Even though I truly loved my first husband, our marriage was, for me, an escape. Desperate, I had hoped my second marriage would be a shelter, but we were like fire and lightning, and the marriage was volatile from the beginning. My constant fear kept me from leaving, and almost three years into the marriage, I found out I was pregnant.

Just one day later, Derek returned home to find me badly injured, and unaware that I was hemorrhaging inside my body. I was in shock and near death when an ambulance arrived to rush me to the hospital.

In the emergency room, I watched as a team of doctors and nurses worked feverishly to save me, attaching monitors and lines, pumping blood into me, and prepping me for emergency surgery. I became aware of the sensation that I was lifting up out of my body. I was able to see them beneath me, working on my body as I looked down over my left shoulder. It didn't make sense to me that no one seemed to notice that I was up above them. I was surprised but not afraid.

I did not go through a tunnel nor see deceased loved ones. Instead, in a moment's time, my life passed in front of me, revealing to me that I had lived my entire life for myself and my loved ones, and not for anyone else, that I had not made any contribution to mankind. I had never thought about my purpose in life before, and now it appeared it would be too late; I assumed I had lived my life doing what I was supposed to do as a human being: caring for myself and those close to me. Thinking about others beyond my own family had never been my concern.

Still floating above everyone, I observed that my pain was gone completely. I heard a kind, soothing voice ask me, "Are you ready to come?"

All of the fears that had held me captive all those years were gone, even now, in the moment of my approaching death. I had the feeling of a deep peace in my heart. It would have been so easy to just say yes.

"I am not afraid to come, but I have a young son." I had the sense that whoever was speaking to me seemed to understand, and then I felt myself lowering back to the bed and into my body, once again to feel pain. I could hear the doctor decide they couldn't wait any longer to operate, so they ran my gurney down the hallway to surgery. I remember noticing a clock in the hall reading 3:00 p.m. I wondered if that would be the end of time for me.

In the room a doctor leaned down to tell me they were going to put me out with gas, saying, "It's okay, just relax." I looked around the room and nodded. I was ready, truly, for whatever the outcome might be. This time, the world would disappear into blackness.

I woke up several hours later. Not only had I survived, but this near-death experience changed me. I had been given a gift that eliminated my crippling fear and gave me a new spiritual perspective that would now direct me, for the rest of my life, to give to the world beyond myself. I still had a long way to go and so much more to experience and learn. It would be fifteen more years before I would meet the Schmitt family, and almost forty-five years later the true irony of what happened to me this day would come full circle, as you will learn in the epilogue.

I do not have all of the answers, spiritually, about what happened to me, nor do I question it. Today, it doesn't matter to me if anyone believes me or understands. I don't know what different religions teach about near-death events; I only know it was the most beautiful experience I have ever had. I no longer fear death because I know what the outcome will be for me.

At the time, I just let it be my own private memory. Like others who have had this experience, I didn't talk about it for a long time. I recuperated and returned home. I had lost the baby and was told it was unlikely I would ever be able to have another child. Two years later, I gave birth to Cory, the best part of my second marriage.

Not long after Cory was born, I had to take my sons and leave my second husband, though we had a shared custody agreement. The three of us started over, but the aftermath of my second broken marriage proved to be more than I could handle. An innocent victim of that period of my life, Cory went back and forth between us for a while, but eventually I had to make the impossible decision to let go of Cory completely, as he approached his twelfth birthday. After my own childhood experience of being abandoned by my birth mother, this situation was devastating. I knew what it felt like, and I knew there would be long-term consequences.

In spite of our complicated relationship, we have spoken and spent time together many times throughout the years and he and his brother love each other and are still in contact. In fact, many years later as a young adult, Cory would come to my rescue when I needed help.

By this time, Derek was in his twenties and on his own. He followed his father's footsteps into the world of music, focusing on stage tech. Derek eventually got married and became a father to a beautiful little girl, my first grandchild.

So now, I was truly alone. While I still had my friends and my work with clients, this was a challenging period in my life. I realized how isolated I had become. At first, I just increased my work hours to fill the time, but after work, I dreaded returning to my now vacant apartment, cooking for one, and maybe watching television. I was healthy and in my mid-thirties. I needed to get out in the world and engage with people. This vulnerability was harder than I thought it would be. I had lost touch with the deepest part of myself. My biggest problem was where to start.

I began having fun, accepting invitations to many different kinds of events. I entered a social world I had never experienced before. I ran myself silly with my newfound friends, some of whom were living lifestyles that didn't sit well with me. I got into outdoor sports like hiking and water skiing, and while it was all exciting, this new life could not fill the void I felt inside. I appeared happy, and men began to ask me out, but after all I had been through, I was trying not to repeat the mistakes of the past. I was looking for true love; of course, I had only experienced that as a giddy seventeen-year-old girl.

Although I was making new friends and Derek and I talked on the phone every Sunday, I never adjusted to returning to an empty apartment. I had to struggle as any single person does.

This is how the next several years went by. Being alone is never more difficult than when you are sick or injured with no one to help you, or pick up the slack, or help with expenses. I had my share of life's traumas that set me back during those years. When you are alone in those situations, you have to pick yourself up and move forward because there is no one to take care of you. This was something I was very good at, something I learned as a young child, and that is exactly what I did—until, by now in my forties, everything changed—again.

My father had also been diagnosed with cancer during this period, and I found myself facing both his illness and my own personal and financial upset, all at the same time. You may know what it's like to live right on the margin, such that any little thing can cause everything to collapse. Coming out of my second-floor apartment one rainy morning, I slipped and tumbled all the way to the bottom of the stairs, hitting my head and landing at an awkward angle. I had whiplash, torn ligaments, a protruded disc, and a fracture in my back. As a result of this fall, I would be in a back brace for many years. It seemed that my short spell of self-sufficiency as a single woman was now coming to an end.

I now had back and neck injuries, which added another shock to my already stressed-out nervous system. A month later, I was back in the hospital for a complete hysterectomy. The recovery from this surgery was the most physically painful experience of my life, compounded by lingering pain from the fall, making even the simplest tasks almost impossible.

The third day after surgery, I went home alone from the hospital to my apartment, anxious to keep any more medical costs from accumulating. But I found I could not take care of myself at all. Exhausted, I was finally able to fall asleep.

The following day, a phone call jarred me out of my rest. My father had died during the night.

I got word to both of my sons that their papaw had died. Cory came to visit me and, seeing that I had not recovered enough to take care of myself yet, stayed about a week to help care for me.

Sharon with her two sons, Cory (left) and Derek (right) 1994. Photo courtesy of the author.

I was devastated by my father's loss and felt that I couldn't take any more trauma. I was ready to give up, just throw in the towel, but again, I didn't have any choice. I would have to manage my own recovery, bury my father, and deal with the aftermath however I could. In extreme post-surgery pain and grieving my father's passing, I wondered what else was going to go wrong. It did not take long to find out.

20

Rescued

1992

For the first year after my fall, I could only work a few hours a day. Most of my hair clients eventually went to other shops, unable to wait for me to serve them. With more money going out than coming in and over twenty thousand dollars in medical debt, my life was quickly falling apart. I had to quit physical therapy and struggle to salvage my credit while I adjusted to the reality that I would experience chronic pain for the rest of my life.

I found myself depressed, lonely, and stressed, lost in a mire of bills. Figuring out how I was supposed to reach out beyond myself to help others was the farthest thing from my mind. I could not even take care of myself. Perhaps like others who have fallen on hard times, who may be reading my story right now, I had to ration the food I ate to pay my bills. I had gas money only for transportation to work. I became leery of people and thought that everybody was out to hurt me. I thought back to my adoptive mother's paranoia and thought, *am I going to suffer the same fate?* With my old fears beginning to circle again, I was in a dark place.

Isolation, depression, and the realization that the social life I had embraced left me empty, abandoned, and more alone than ever before, all brought me to my knees in prayer, and eventually led me back to church, and one step closer to the Schmitt family. After visiting several churches without feeling like I belonged, a friend suggested I visit Southeast Christian Church, a large church on the east end of Louisville, thinking I might find the answers to my prayers there.

As I entered the church that first Sunday, I saw that all the people had happy faces, which instilled me with hope once again. I wanted *that*. Being there gave me the incentive to go on with my life and develop a new identity based on my connection to God.

As the minister, Bob Russell, began his sermon that Sunday, I felt like it was written just for me and my concerns, but that's how God works. On any given Sunday in any given church, people listening to the sermon will feel God's presence and sense he is speaking directly to them. I immediately grasped the underlying meaning of his sermon: forgiveness would be the key to pushing forward. I certainly had a lot of people to forgive, including myself.

This service was a very transformative experience, and I decided to keep attending. Over the next few weeks, others noticed the changes in my attitude and life, people who were also searching for what I had found. Friends and clients started attending church with me.

I was amazed that a preacher I did not know could stand in a pulpit and seemingly directly address someone like me, someone with severe, complex problems, with just the right message. Yet, while I heard the familiar themes of love and forgiveness, it was the Spirit flowing through the message that electrified me.

I gained new strength to carry out the hard work of straightening out my life. Feeling better about myself and my prospects, I made some dents in my bleak financial situation. Things were definitely looking up.

One Sunday, I closed my eyes during the sermon and went to a deep place. There, I realized how my recent traumas had clouded a spirituality that had once bolstered me. I remembered the foundation of faith I found in my youth through my neighborhood angel, Dorothy. I thought about my biological mother's connection to her church, which had both hurt me and given me a way to connect with her. And then, of course, the revelations of my near-death experience reminded me of the reality of the hereafter—and of my responsibilities here on earth. This renewal of faith helped restore me and give me the strength to deal with my problems.

Eventually, I found a singles Sunday school class named Passages, taught by Ralph Dennison. He was one of the most motivating teachers I had ever encountered. I later accepted a class leadership position that led me to enroll in the church's Care Ministry training.

I trained with a minister of Southeast named Richard Shanks, an excellent teacher who understood what others were feeling. Richard and the loving people of this class restored my belief in myself, and showed me that I could be most fruitful by helping others.

It is odd how things work out, but as we were taught in Sunday school class, everything happens for a reason. Now I understood that, had I not had my difficult life experiences, I would not have known how to help others shed their pain. And, had I not had my near-death experience, I would not have had that desire for a purpose in my life bigger than my own needs. I would never have said yes that unusually cool Kentucky August morning as I read about the Schmitt family.

The care ministry seemed like the perfect way for me to give back to others, to lead them to an understanding of how God can help us through our many trials, like what I suffered. *With faith and a little encouragement from me,* I believed, *they could also overcome their hardships.* I would learn soon enough that sometimes people need more than faith and a little encouragement, and that often, our service to others will do more for us than we ever could do for them. I had a lot to learn.

It is not always easy to confront the problems within us, but the walk becomes easier once we take the first step. We often realize that we are not as alone as we thought and that others have suffered similar misfortunes. The way back from those problems required faith in God and surrendering my will to his.

I urge people who live with hate and deep wounds to seek the counsel of someone who deeply cares for others. We have to understand that transformation has to start somewhere, and it's up to us to take that first step.

The Care Ministry training I received reinforced my belief in the essence of who I was, despite what I had been through. I realized that I was on the right path, and earned the confidence of the church ministers, who contributed to my spiritual growth.

What I learned most of all was that the greatest gift I received was also the greatest gift I could give: helping others, especially those in deep pain. The timing of my return to my faith was nothing short of God's perfect plan. If I ever doubted that I was supposed to accept the greatest challenge of my life, a task so far out of my reach that only God and his host of earthly angels could accomplish it, I only had to look to this moment. It was my attendance at Southeast and my completion of their Care Ministry training that put me on the phone with Chuck Lee, who could tell me about Theresa's death that morning, encourage me to act, and put me in touch with the family.

Everything that had happened to me in my life, every hard lesson, every painful step, every act of mercy and grace, was intersecting with my new path that would carry me from this point forward.

What I could not know yet was that God had brought me through so much, not so that I could be part of his plan to rescue Michelle, but so that he could use this beautiful little child to rescue *me*.

We were at a critical point in our mission to save Michelle, who had only a short time left to live unless she received a new liver. We could do a lot of things for her, but in order for her to survive, someone else would have to lose their life. Someone's loved one would have to make the decision to donate their organs. This sacrifice put everything we were doing in perspective.

21

One Step Back

SEPTEMBER 18, 1993

As our fundraising efforts grew, I continued to visit the girls, building a close relationship with them, their father, and grandparents, and having fun together. It was so important to me that the girls knew I loved them, and that the family knew they could trust me and that I had only the best motives. Ashley was always glad to see me, and Michelle would join in to share some quality time with us, as best she could, given that she rarely felt well.

Once, on my way back from a donation jar pickup, I stopped by their house and was inspired to bring the jar inside. The girls' eyes popped wide open as I dumped the money on a coffee table. Ashley and I separated the paper money into stacks while Michelle stacked rows of pennies, dimes, and quarters.

Barbara took a few dollars and went to the grocery store; she came back with a half-gallon of ice cream that we devoured. Of course, Michelle could only eat so much, but the whole experience seemed to bond us closer.

Afterward, Michelle was finally comfortable enough with me to come close and lovingly pat my hand, a very big step forward. Then Barbara brought out the girls' coloring books, and Michelle sat in my lap and pointed out the pictures she had colored. Then we colored some together. For being such a young girl, Ashley was very chatty and comfortable talking to me; Michelle, now two, still was not talking, to me or anyone else. She would express herself through her face, still only making sounds to indicate "yes" or "no."

That night she held my hand and walked me to the door as I was leaving. After that, Michelle would come to the door with Ashley to greet me on my visits. She always seemed excited to see me and would immediately join in.

I continued to work with Millie Sola, writing stories and designing ads for *Entertainer Magazine*, our primary outreach to the public after the hair-a-thon. But, as I said, Millie and I were like the Odd Couple, working together but living in two different worlds. This added some "drag" to our collaboration.

Money was coming in, but too little and too slowly. Our articles encouraged businesses to do some fundraisers on their own, but I decided to put together a benefit concert—more than that, a huge, day-long, outdoor music festival. This would prove to be another case where, had I known what would be involved, I probably would not have tried it.

My first husband, Wayne Young, by now a well-known blues guitarist with a beautiful wife and family, had exposed me to "big time" concert shows during our short marriage many years before. We went on two road show tours with Dick Clark, and other tours as well, where I witnessed all aspects of concert production. Since we were still good friends, I gave Wayne a call. He should have known better than to pick up the phone.

Given that this was to be a fundraising event, Wayne took on the challenge of getting bands and solo artists to donate their performances to the cause. My son, Derek, provided lighting, a professional sound system, and the manpower and expertise that would allow the artists to perform at their best.

The production had to be perfect, and I enjoyed this once-in-a-lifetime opportunity to work together with Wayne and Derek.

Millie and I went into full gear to promote this upcoming fundraiser. After Millie secured the location at Churchill Downs, Louisville's famous home to the Kentucky Derby, posters would go up in nightclubs, restaurants, churches, and grocery stores. By this time, Michelle's condition was getting worse. Her grandmother commented, "She is suffering a lot more than I ever saw Ashley suffer."

Millie wrote updates about Michelle's deteriorating condition in the magazine. Up to this point we had raised less than $50,000. This big benefit concert was to be our best chance to perhaps double or triple that amount, still well short of my half-million-dollar goal, but a big boost that would also raise awareness for the community once again.

While Millie negotiated the arrangements for the site, I continued to set things up, calling the performers and their managers and providing out-of-towners with accommodations. I also checked with Derek daily on the production details.

We drew on regional performers who were aware of our mission and glad to participate, including Wayne Young and his band. Everything seemed to be falling into place, and the technicians were ready to set up once we had a firm location and a concert date.

I kept pressuring Millie to finalize her location plans, and she gave me a date that she also advertised on the front page of her magazine. I relayed the details to the 150 people involved. Many would take leave from paid positions to work this benefit concert.

As it turned out, Millie's booking at Churchill Downs was not confirmed at all. Time was running out and the pressure was on to deliver the specifications for the stage setup. With only days to go, Millie finally found the courage to tell me that Churchill Downs was unable to let us do the event there. As it turned out, she explained that her contact was not authorized to set this up. I called the man in charge and explained our situation. While he sympathized with us, another event was scheduled for that date. With less than three weeks to go, we had to find another venue.

I could have died and crawled in a hole. I had a full production ready to go, a date that could not be moved, publicity set in motion, performers who had rearranged schedules, but no stage. Millie was devastated, but we had to salvage our concert.

I immediately made calls to other locations, explaining our need for a stage and auditorium. At this late date, prime venues were all booked. Some sympathetic managers called around, but nobody could move their dates. Finally, I was able to rent space at the Kentucky Fair and Expo Center's secondary venue, but we had a huge obstacle.

Angels, Inc. had run out of money needed to pay for the space rental, much less front all of the attractions we had booked to draw people in. We had a car show, rides, and bands ready to play the event, but my expenses exceeded our funds.

This state property would be costly to use, and I had already invested all of my own money. There was nothing left; I might have to cancel the event. I went back to the Hurstbourne Kiwanis club, and they gave me another generous donation, but it still wasn't enough.

I was facing our first fundraising failure and dreaded making the cancellation announcement. I was preparing the press release when I took a break to pick up mail from our post office box. There I found the sweetest letter from Mary Bingham, who owned the *Courier-Journal* at the time. She had enclosed a check for the exact amount of money needed to go forward with the event. Mary was truly a godsend that day.

The benefit event was on, but we still had obstacles. This location was behind the horse barns and hidden from the highway and entrance road. The night before the concert, some radio and television stations did broadcast our benefit concert's relocation, and Jim Adams managed to write another feature article about the event for the *Courier-Journal*, published a couple of days before.

Today, this same location is home to some of the largest concert events in the state, but at that time, even the guards at the front gate booth didn't know where to direct people arriving for the concert. I got a lot of angry calls the next day from disappointed people.

The concert itself went off without a hitch. The production ran smoothly, and those who made it there were thrilled by the performances. All the artists were at their very best, and Wayne made a special appearance and rocked, as they say. I was extremely proud of my son, Derek, whose hard-earned experience producing musical events like this was truly put to the test.

In the days after the concert, I was exhausted and felt I had let the Schmitts down. In spite of the huge mistakes we had made, we still managed to cover costs and raise some money for Michelle's operation; however, we could have done so much better. I felt frustrated and discouraged, and I began to doubt myself. What business did I have taking on such an enormous mission?

22

Number One Spot

DECEMBER 1993

Michelle was getting worse by the day, enduring one hospital stay after another as complications began to occur. It was sad to see her in this condition, but it inspired me to move faster. The sicker she got, the more the medical costs grew. We struggled to raise enough money to keep the spiraling costs at bay, but what Michelle really needed was a liver. Time was running out.

I was so thankful that Barbara was there for the girls. She was a wonderful caregiver as well as a loving grandma. She had learned about medication and worked out a precise schedule for administering the complicated combinations of pills and shots.

But Barbara was showing signs of being run down herself. My concern for the family's health now included her. She had dark circles under her eyes that sunk into her cheekbones. I suggested that she see a doctor, but she wouldn't hear of it.

"No, I'll be okay. And I can't leave Michelle for a minute, especially now," she explained.

Shortly afterward, Barbara caught a virus, and Ed had to take the girls while she recovered. I stopped by every day to help out but could see that Ashley had pitched in and was keeping Michelle busy. We played some games together, and I fixed dinner a couple of nights.

I reassured the girls that their grandmother just caught a flu virus and would soon recover. They knew me well enough to trust my word, but I could also see that Michelle was getting weaker, her skin even more yellowish. I could only pray that the call would come soon.

This unknown factor put a lot of stress on the family, not knowing when they would need to fly to Omaha, or *if* a donor liver would arrive in time. With Barbara's return, the Schmitt family was totally housebound due to Michelle's low viral and bacterial resistance. Even a cold could push her over the edge.

Finding the right donor match at the time the person needs it is a challenging task. The new liver has to be a perfect match for blood and tissue type; otherwise, the body will reject it. Generally, it's a very long wait, and many patients waiting for a liver don't make it. The more time passed, the closer we came to losing Michelle. I could not bear the thought, instead focusing my energies on things I could do to help.

It was hard to pray for a donor liver. For a liver to be found, at that time, another human being would have to pass away. Would there be someone out there who would lose their life, a family who would have to say goodbye to their loved one, while Michelle received the gift of life? This is what happened with Ashley, but it was growing more and more impossible for Michelle.

A further complication was the twelve-hour window the surgeons had given to get Michelle to the hospital in Omaha once a donor liver became available. The flight time between Louisville and Omaha for a nonstop charter jet, combined with transportation to and from both airports, and the time it would take to prepare the jet and get the family to the airport meant we had no more than six hours to get her in the air when, or *if*, we got the call.

Michelle also had to be completely healthy at the time of her surgery. The doctors would postpone the surgery even if she had a sniffle. In that case, her new liver would go to someone else, which would be a death sentence at this point for the little girl.

Michelle's itching became worse as she constantly scratched herself. Even today, doctors aren't entirely sure what causes the itching in liver disease. However, some research indicates that it is due to the higher levels of bile salt accumulating under the skin, which also causes the jaundiced skin color.

To watch a baby suffer like this is truly horrible. Despite what

Michelle endured, she remained well behaved and fairly uncomplaining. She and Ashley were such good children, despite their illness or the attention given to them.

By December 1993, Michelle had turned three years old, yet only weighed twenty-two pounds, the average weight of a healthy eleven-month-old baby. Her tiny liver continued to enlarge, causing a host of severe conditions, including spontaneous bleeding from her colon and other parts of her body.

Her health was further aggravated by strong medications that ate away at her soft intestinal tissues. She developed vitamin deficiencies from poor absorption, causing her bones to become brittle and easily broken. She developed rickets. Michelle had spells where she could no longer support her weight to stand up.

Her doctors started blood transfusions to aid her overtaxed heart. Then one evening Michelle started bleeding from her nose, requiring an ambulance run to the hospital. Later that week, she sustained a second bleeding episode from the nose. Once again, this required a hospital visit.

Spontaneous bleeding happens in many cases of liver failure, especially in young children. This is due to blood coagulation disorders and complications that can cause hemorrhaging, and can be fatal if they happen somewhere the bleeding cannot quickly be stopped.

This was scary for all of us, but the family was holding up well. When I stopped by, I could see how Michelle's quickly deteriorating condition impacted Barbara, threatened with the sudden death of her granddaughter. I felt helpless but continued to support and encourage them.

When the doctors in Omaha were alerted about Michelle's bleeding episodes, they immediately moved her up to the number one spot on their liver transplant list. This response was encouraging, but we all wondered if she would survive the wait to find a liver match for her surgery.

Barbara carried a special pager that kept her connected directly to the hospital in Omaha. It did sound off on one occasion but was a false alarm. That was scary, but at least we knew that the system worked. We had a few nervous laughs about it, which helped with the building tension.

Most of the family's clothes were packed, but now Barbara and Ed would complete most of the more detailed packing. I also went on alert and contacted the jet team participants to do what was needed to prepare for the call to action.

As I mentioned earlier, Captain Jason Smith, chief pilot for Jim Patterson's plane, had shown great interest in our mission. He seemed to take this off-duty call to save this little girl's life as a personal responsibility.

Captain Smith called consistently throughout the two-year wait, deeply concerned about Michelle's condition. I could feel his sincerity and put him in touch with Barbara, who introduced him over the phone to Ashley, since Michelle still didn't speak.

He was so kind and assured the family of his willingness to transport them to Omaha and do what it took to clear that. He so wanted to fly Michelle and her family there that we put him first of the four on the list. It was very touching to see a grown man this concerned about a child's plight.

The KFC Corporation was second in line to be called, should Mr. Patterson's plane be in use and unavailable at the time. KFC had also shown great interest in Michelle's case. Their restaurants were the top collectors of our donation jars across the state.

My hair client Rick Laughlin, KFC's director of corporate services, who was responsible for scheduling the corporate jet, along with manager Chris Benson, were also constantly in touch with us. They were exceptional people and gave me advice throughout our ordeal on preparing for Michelle's emergency "flight to life," as we called it.

It was an honor to receive support from these busy people and their companies. Airline service entails constant equipment and flight checks, whether commercial jumbo jets or private corporate jets. I had no idea how important it was for them to stay on top of all the details with me about our communication and backup flight plans.

They were used to providing service and dealing with tight and sometimes impossible schedules. As our window of time to help Michelle grew tighter and tighter, the jet team and their staff were alerted and on call, waiting on us. They also expected us to be able to deal with last-minute changes, given our six-hour window.

We were all in position, ready to carry out our lifesaving responsibilities. I had listened to my jet teams' contingency advice over
and over, and thought I was well prepared. What I did not plan for,
what none of us anticipated, showed up the evening of January 16,
1994.

Later, this would remind me of Proverbs 16:9: "The mind
of man plans his way, but the LORD directs his steps." In this case, I
would need some divine stepping stones to get Michelle to Omaha
on time.

23

Frozen City

In real time, trying to beat the clock with such a medical emergency can certainly slow time down, especially when a child's life hangs in the balance. Minutes seem like hours; one hour feels like six; one day feels like a week. Intricate planning was essential, but we couldn't plan beyond a week or two in advance because of Michelle's fragile condition.

Any complication to slow us down further and make the flight to Omaha more difficult would be intolerable. Yet, for whatever divine reason, our team had to face and overcome one more giant obstacle to this child's liver transplant.

As we approached January 16, 1994, weather forecasters had predicted an ice storm, to be followed by anywhere from a wintry mix to heavy snow, with sub-zero temperatures expected the next day. The community had enough notice to prepare to be stuck at home for a couple of days while the city dug out. Like everyone else, I gathered essentials at the grocery store and was almost looking forward to a couple of days to myself, reading and binge-watching the television. As the ice began to fall, we could do nothing but wait for the doctor's call, as we had been doing for two years. The Angels were as prepared as we could be to enable Michelle and her family to make a quick evacuation. Nothing was going to stand in the way of our rescue mission for her. I was not particularly worried that night—at least, not for Michelle.

Louisville will never forget January 16, 1994, for its historic snowfall and freezing temperatures. Weather forecasts predicted seven to fifteen inches of snow for this region of Kentucky. By the end of the day, the snowfall would break the all-time accumulation record and was packed on top of an inch or two of deadly ice. This blizzard brought the entire city to a standstill and created emergencies for businesses and families, including mine.

Some businesses closed early as the emergency broadcasts recommended, and people hurried to get home Sunday afternoon as the storm worsened. Many grocery stores stayed open late for people still needing to stock up for the predicted closures once the storm hit.

People were glued to their televisions, waiting for weather and emergency updates to guide them. The onslaught at grocery stores for food and hardware stores for supplies like lanterns, shovels, and snow blowers would soon empty the shelves. Latecomers would find themselves out of basics like bread, canned food, and milk.

The city silently waited for the snow and freezing rain. By six thirty that night, the streets of Louisville were utterly empty. Soon ice-coated telephone and electrical lines, some snapping in the wind from the weight of the ice, would interrupt essential services.

I was home that evening, looking out my window while I listened to the news. I was hoping my son Derek would arrive soon. Derek had recently moved in with me, working hard to save money and get back on his feet after his marriage fell apart. Derek was running tech for a gig that night. *Surely the gig will be canceled,* I thought.

Around 7:00 p.m., the mayor sent out an emergency mandate for citizens to stay at home and that we all might be homebound as long as three days. This standstill would be like a mini-vacation for me, but there was an underlying feeling of concern for my own family and for the Schmitts. As conditions worsened, I just had to wait and see, like everyone else. There was nothing else to do.

Around 11:00 p.m., everything turned instantly critical for my own family. I got a call that Derek's truck had broken down on the way back from his concert gig, and he was stranded. His ex-wife gave me a general location, but the street names she gave didn't make sense to me. I tried calling back but got no answer.

As I looked outside, the street was already covered in ice. I waited for a call from my son, praying for his safe return. I watched the news and learned that the weather conditions were getting worse by the moment.

Emergency alerts continued broadcasting, pleading with people to avoid any travel. Yet, I still had not heard from Derek, stranded in a broken-down car, and I was gravely concerned for his safety.

By midnight, over sixty thousand homes were without electricity and heat, the numbers rising by the hour as the temperature dropped further. Fallen live wires on the streets were another hazard for anyone still on the road. Icy precipitation had begun to change over to thick, wet snow.

Shelters were opened at schools and community centers to accommodate those without power. Alerts went out to everyone with four-wheel-drive vehicles to help transport people to shelters and assist emergency services ferrying the sick to hospitals or delivering critical blood supplies.

By this time, Governor Brereton Jones had held a press conference, announcing only emergency vehicles and those bringing in food supplies, clearing roads, or towing vehicles would be allowed on the freeways. Many trucks and vehicles were already stuck, cluttering these highways and making them impassable. The Red Cross was in the process of rescuing people, including young children, from those stranded cars.

January 16, 1994, was one of the longest evenings of my life, my concern for Derek compounded by Michelle's worsening condition. At least we had power. While I awaited a call from Derek or the sound of his return home, I considered disobeying the governor's emergency orders and driving out in search of my son. But, I had no idea where he would be. I could picture him out there in the blizzard, stranded and maybe freezing, and I was unable to reach him.

While Derek was very levelheaded and resourceful, everything in the city was closed down, the streets deserted. I could just imagine him knocking on doors and asking for shelter and wondered if he would find it.

Worries about his safety raced through my mind. Derek was my son but also my best friend. He had made sacrifices, just as I had, to help establish Angels, Inc. We had been through so much together.

Around 3:00 a.m., Derek all but fell through the front door. His coat was covered in ice, his face blistered from the cold and wind. His hair was gnarled and frozen with slivers of ice and snow, his work clothes frozen stiff. He was truly a sight but also a sight for sore eyes. I was so relieved to see him.

After removing his frozen coat, he sat down on the couch, his hands trembling, his lips quivering, coughing out, "I walked all the way back. Nobody on the roads." I had thrown a blanket over his shivering body and heated water for hot chocolate. He slowly sipped from the steaming cup.

"Derek, I was so afraid for you. Why didn't you call? I would have driven out to you!"

"I tried, but the first two pay phones were out, and so I just decided to trudge my way home. And there's no way I would let you try to drive in that storm!"

After some time, Derek came around a bit, then retreated to take a hot bath while I fixed some chicken noodle soup, the old standby for quick, hot nourishment. After he changed into dry clothes, we sat at the kitchen table while he ate his soup.

Derek had walked over ten miles to get home, nearly succumbing to the city's bleak conditions. During his long trek through this strange, record-breaking blizzard, he told me he saw only one car on the road the entire night. "Not even a police car or an ambulance I could flag down," he lamented.

Faced with a deserted city and no rescue in sight, he was on his own to get home safely, trudging through ice-coated streets and sidewalks, with snow falling so hard he couldn't see ahead of him as the wind pummeled him and drove the temperature lower and lower. Derek understood the danger and felt truly blessed he made it home under these circumstances.

As I went upstairs to go to bed about four in the morning, I lay there thinking about my son out in this dangerous weather and wondered how close he had come to freezing to death. I thought about Ed Schmitt and his worries about Michelle surviving long enough to get her lifesaving liver transplant, which put everything in perspective for me. Both Ed and I would do anything to save our children. Both of us were in the anguishing position where there was nothing we could do but wait. I had to wait less than twelve hours to know Derek was safe; Ed Schmitt and his parents had been waiting like this for three agonizing *years*.

As I laid my head down on my pillow, Michelle was on my mind. I ran through all the details about how we would get her to Omaha when her call came. Had we forgotten anything? With Derek safe and asleep downstairs, this was my only real concern. *No*, I thought to myself. *Everything else is in place. We are organized to perfection.* I was secure in knowing our jet team was ready to whisk Michelle away to a new liver and a new life. There was nothing for me to worry about, or so I thought. I fell asleep about 4:30 a.m.

I woke up late the next morning as the sun began to shine.

24

Snow Angels

MONDAY, JANUARY 17, 1994

When I was called to this mission two years earlier, sitting at my kitchen table reading that news article, I dedicated the task to God and pledged myself to grow it into whatever it needed to be. The overwhelming, heartfelt response from the community gave rise to the Angels, Inc. nonprofit organization, which we dedicated to helping other children in need once Michelle's family was taken care of.

Initially, twelve people came forward to launch our "Angels" mission. Whether we had twelve or two or two hundred, it wouldn't have mattered. I'll just quote Matthew 18 verse 20: "For where two or three have gathered together in My name, I am there in their midst." In the end, we had thousands, and God was certainly in our midst.

Many of these people were not what you would call religious, but whether they knew it or would admit as much, they were directed by something spiritual. They became God's ordinary angels. Whether we believe in God or not, he is in the spark kindled within all of us when we respond to the needy, in our backyard, or across the globe.

It was natural for me to put my trust and faith in God. Throughout my life, I have seen the miracles that happen when we call upon God, whom I believe was with us every step of the way during our mission. Again, others might not have seen it that way, but as they say, "God works in mysterious ways."

That day, our little group was about to witness another miracle. When it came right down to it, in the moment when Michelle most needed our help, we were helpless; our selfless Louisville community was about to step in and do the impossible. As everything unfolded, I couldn't help but think of Michelle's dear mother. Was she pleading for her family before God in that moment, opening the doors of heaven for us? Everything seemed to happen at the worst possible time in our human understanding, but also with perfect timing from God's viewpoint.

We all wanted to give Michelle a chance at a quality life, just as we did with our children. As the events of this day unfolded, newscasts about our community's effort to save this child in a race against time, in a frozen city of ice and snow, would reach the farthest corners of the planet.

9:30 a.m.—6 hours to liftoff

I woke up to a bright sunny morning with a brisk chill in the air, yet with a subdued stillness everywhere. Walking down the stairs, I saw out the window that the snowstorm had subsided. Still drowsy, I prepared a cup of coffee. The silence was cozy and the room unusually bright, augmented by the sunshine reflected through the windows off of the white landscape outside.

The coffee aroma surrounded me in my small kitchen as I yawned and stretched to wake up. Sipping my coffee, I thought I had better see how much snow we received. My ground-level view was much different than looking down at it from upstairs.

I was astonished and had to rub my eyes and look again. The accumulation outside our door was nineteen inches. It looked like the bottom of the surrounding houses was cut off, as was the lower half of my car. The mailbox was totally covered by drifts that had blown up against every surface. This was more snow than I had ever seen in my life.

The night before, I remembered musing about enjoying a weather vacation amidst all the recent turmoil. What more could you ask for but to be snowed in for a week, with plenty of food in the cupboard? So I sat at the kitchen table, viewing the trees covered with icy crystals majestically glistening as if in a fairyland, and relaxed a bit.

I watched for the squirrels outside my window that generally ran up and down the trees. They weren't out today, but I didn't worry about them since they had stocked away food for the winter. I saw a few squirrels looking out of their high tree nests, probably just as shocked about the snowdrifts.

Then, at 9:30 a.m., the phone rang.

It was a friend of Barbara, the girls' grandmother, telling me that Michelle's call had come from Omaha. The clock was ticking, and we only had six hours to get her there. By "there," she meant we had six hours to get her in the air and on her way.

• • •

IN REAL TIME, the surgeons had twelve hours from the moment the liver donor passed away to transplant the liver into Michelle's tiny body. They would need two hours or more to prep Michelle for surgery. The flight could take as long as two and a half hours in good conditions, and it would take thirty minutes to get her off the plane, to a waiting ambulance, to the hospital, and then to the right location within the hospital. Michelle would need to be airborne no later than 3:30 p.m. Louisville time; we had six hours to get her in the air.

• • •

I AUTOMATICALLY WENT into high gear and immediately called Barbara to verify that information. While this was the moment we had all been waiting for after two long, tedious years, it couldn't have come at a worse time, with us and our transport plane buried in snow. Not only was phone service spotty throughout the city, but after all of this preparation, after everything I had worked so hard to make happen, I would be unable to dash over to the Schmitt home to help with the girls in these last critical hours. I would have to be content to do whatever I could from my phone and then let others step in to help the family in my place. This was excruciating, but all for the best. Michelle and her family truly belonged to the people of Louisville now and to a growing support community around the world. Soon enough, I would have to completely let go of this family I had grown so fond of; but for now, there was a lot of work still to be done.

When I talked with Barbara, there was a lot of stress in her voice; her tone worried me. She verified that the hospital had called, but she added hesitantly, "Ed is ready to turn down the liver because of the snow and getting there on time."

I immediately asked, "Have you called Jason?" Jason was our first choice for a pilot and would be our first call.

"Yes, and he said he's going to try to do it if he can get out of his driveway, which is packed with snow."

I knew that nothing, especially mounds of snow, was going to prevent Jason Smith from helping this child. His personal interest in her welfare came from the heart. Like mine, his promise to help was more like a fictitious vow given by medieval knights in a storybook.

Jason Smith assured me he and his airplane were going to be ready to fly, so we just had to get millions of pounds of snow removed from the airport runway. We also had to get Michelle and her family safely and quickly to that airport through iced-over and impassable city streets.

I told Barbara, "Just keep packing unless you hear from me. And tell Ed, I'm going to get the family to Omaha no matter what."

After hanging up from talking to Barbara, I first called the storm command center at the mayor's office. They needed to know what we planned to do, and we needed any assistance they could give us.

A nice lady answered the phone. "This is the mayor's office. May I help you?" Little did this young lady realize the kind of "help" I was asking for: a mammoth snow removal operation at the airport.

"This is Sharon Stevens of Angels, Inc. As you may have heard, we are responsible for the arrangements to fly Michelle Schmitt, a two-year-old liver transplant patient, to Omaha for her surgery." I took a deep breath. "That call came at nine this morning, and we've got six hours to get her there [to the airport]."

"My God," she said. "Today? With all this snow on the ground?"

"Yes," I said and went on to explain. "This was a prearranged project within the Louisville community with hundreds of volunteers. But, of course, we didn't expect this snowstorm."

It took her a moment to shift gears. "You need to talk to the Crisis Outreach Center."

"Who are they?" I asked.

"Just call WHAS Radio."

Mary Jeffries, the assistant news director and drive-time anchor at WHAS Radio, answered the phone. I repeated the same message I gave the mayor's office. This station was covering our weather crisis and working with a skeleton crew. They had been on the air all morning putting out information, connecting people who needed help with those who could assist with four-wheel drives, information about shelters, or whatever they might need. Mary listened to what I had to say.

Afterward, there was a brief silence before she came back and said, "We're going to pull this off." She rapidly asked several questions, clarifying what I had just told her.

10:30 a.m.—5 hours to lift-off

An hour later, Mary asked me to go on air with her to announce this appeal to the community. During that time she had done her due diligence to confirm the details, and sent a news crew, Beth Merrill and Ron Robertson, over to the Schmitts' house in their four-wheel drive.

On air, I relayed the call for help: "We have a little girl who is to receive a liver transplant. About an hour and a half ago she received her call to be in Omaha. She has six hours to get there." Radio DJ John Asher asked his listening audience for ideas.

By this time, in reality, she had just five hours left to be in the air. Standiford Field was closed and not expected to open until 5:00 p.m. or later, but a crew and volunteers were already using heavy equipment to prepare one runway for this life-or-death situation. Our pilot, Jason Smith, and his copilot, Jeff Bowman, were working their way to the airfield in a four-wheel-drive police car, which amazingly was parked next door. As soon as they arrived at the airport, they would begin to prepare the jet for takeoff.

The response was overwhelming. Many people in the listening audience had heard about Michelle and her situation from fundraisers that had been going on the past two years and were already glued to their radios during this weather crisis. As this mass of helpers headed out, Hank Wagner and David Fleming of Jewish Hospital made their Skycare helicopter available to ferry the family to the airport or to another standby jet, but they needed a flight nurse and paramedic on board to make the transport. Getting them picked up and on the helicopter was proving to be difficult. The *Courier-Journal* later reported that flight nurse Rick Nickoson drove his own four-wheel drive to pick up paramedic Joe Vetter for the trip.

Like everyone else, the Schmitt family and their two girls woke up to the sight of snow-covered lawns and streets. Neither of them had ever seen so much snow. Ashley couldn't wait to get dressed and stomp around outside. This was cut short by the hospital's call.

Barbara got everybody moving in the right direction. Then, suddenly, there came a knock on the door. Ed opened it to find WHAS radio newscasters Beth Merrill and Ron Robertson on their doorstep, ready to help out.

After they stomped off their snowy shoes, Barbara brought them inside and turned the living room into their own crisis center. She called me, and I talked everyone through what was going to have to happen.

First, we needed an airport runway cleared of snow so the Learjet could take off. The mayor's office was working with the airport authority to make this happen, but the jet had to be prepared, and the crew had to make it to the airport on time.

Next, we needed to get the family safely to the airport. A helicopter could get Michelle and one other person to the airport, but her family would still have to be brought in, either by another helicopter or by four-wheel drive, and the helicopter would need a place near the Schmitt home to land. The News Radio 840 WHAS road team set up a remote feed to the station, both audio and video. Their broadcasts would get the whole community involved.

1:00 p.m.—2 ½ hours to liftoff

The station manager put me on the air again around 1:00 p.m., asking questions about Michelle's condition, about what happened to her mother and sister, what the family's financial needs were, and where to donate. Ed and Barbara were very nervous, thankful but surprised that our "Angel Flight" preparations had gelled so quickly after the Omaha hospital call.

But, I could hear the trepidation in her voice. I had to reassure her. "It's all arranged. We even have a backup out of Cincinnati. So we're getting Michelle there no matter what."

Barbara's sigh revealed her relief, mixed with stress. She cleared her throat and then added one request, "We want Jason for our pilot."

I said gently, "Don't worry. He will be there. I just know he will." I could give her plenty of assurances, but my confidence was built on faith, not on solid information. Everything that was happening at this point was well out of my hands.

While workers and volunteers were already on the ground working to clear the airport runway, we had another problem. The helicopter would need a safe place to land near the Schmitts' home, and we would need a safe way to transport Michelle and her family to the helicopter.

25

Ninety Minutes

2:00 P.M.

2:00 p.m.—90 minutes to lift-off

WHAS Radio broadcast the need out to the community asking for ideas, and one woman who lived nearby, Teresa Amshoff, had a great one. She could see a huge, snow-covered, empty parking lot right outside her door—the church parking lot for Southeast Christian Church, which in 1994 was on Hikes Lane in Louisville, could be cleared for a helicopter to land, and it was close to the Schmitt family's home.

She called the radio station, who relayed the information to those working on the details for the mission. Beth Merrill asked her, "Can you get people there to clear off a landing pad?"

"Yes," she answered, and the plan was in place. While Teresa and her husband, Joe, ran out into the neighborhood, pounding doors to rally help, WHAS broadcast the need out to the community. Dave Stone, one of the pastors of the church, happened to be walking up to the building at the very moment the first volunteer showed up. With his five-year-old daughter Savannah in tow, Dave had decided to relieve their cabin fever by getting some work done at the church, completely unaware of the miracle that was about to unfold. "Where are we supposed to go?" a man with a shovel called out to him. Dave remembers the scene vividly:

That caught me a little off guard, especially since he was car-rying a shovel. He explained to me about the announcement that had been made on the radio and television, that a land-ing area needed to be cleared for a helicopter to transport a girl who desperately needed a liver transplant.

The fact that I had a key to the building evidently gave me some kind of credibility! I helped locate the area farthest from any electrical wires. One of the first gentlemen to join us, Joe Amshoff, stepped off a square for us to shovel. As we started, neighbors continued to walk up and dive in to help.

Once they got started I went to the facilities area to get more shovels. I also went to retrieve a huge blue tarp. My think-ing was the bright color could serve as a visible landing spot from the air. Ten minutes later my daughter and I returned to an ever growing group of volunteers. Neighbors had been joined by Southeast church members and others in the area who had 4-wheel drive vehicles. Eventually, a fire truck, and even a snowplow showed up to help.

The snow was deep, but soon we had over a hundred people involved, and were able to get a large spot cleared. Here were all of these people working together. Everyone was propelled by the cause and working side by side with people who had just spontaneously responded to meet a need.

While the volunteers worked, the next phase of our operation was getting Michelle, her sister, father, grandmother, and all of their luggage to the parking lot. WHAS Radio's four-wheel-drive van was sitting out front of the Schmitts' home. They agreed to trans-port the Schmitt family to the helicopter pickup site at the South-east Christian Church parking lot. It was one and a half miles away through snow and ice-covered streets. The Schmitt family and all of their luggage piled into the WHAS vehicle with Beth and Ron, Michelle held tightly on Barbara's lap. As they made their way carefully down the road to the church, the helicopter crew took off from Jewish Hospital to meet them there. About forty-five minutes after Teresa first called in, the spot where the helicopter could land was cleared, and volunteers had almost finished clearing the path needed to get the transport vehicle to the helicopter.

2:45 p.m.—45 minutes to liftoff

Within just a few minutes after the landing pad and driveway were cleared, the helicopter landed, and the family pulled into the parking lot. Dave Stone recalls this dramatic moment:

When the helicopter came in sight, we felt this blend of tension and excitement. We were concerned that everything would go smoothly with the helicopter landing and subsequent trip to Nebraska and surgery, but there was also an optimism that this was going to come together, that somehow God was intervening, and he was using a community to help make it happen.

As the helicopter descended, everyone suddenly realized the huge blue tarp marking the landing spot was not the wisest idea. While it helped the helicopter pilot find us, the tarp was so light that it started blowing around and quickly became a hazard. We got rid of it. (Whose stupid idea was that?)

No sooner had the helicopter landed then a man emerged out of a vehicle carrying a little girl in a blue winter coat. You could tell she wasn't feeling very well and didn't have a lot of strength. Watching them get in the helicopter was a profound moment for all of us. I reacted especially strongly as I held my own daughter in my arms, who was just a little older than Michelle.

The crowd burst into applause as they lifted off. It wasn't just the helicopter that ascended. At that same moment we were all sending prayers heavenward for that little girl who we didn't know but for some reason we now felt connected to.

Within minutes, the helicopter was on the way to Standiford

Airport with Michelle and her grandmother, and the family was on the way in the WHAS vehicle.

By this time, less than an hour remained for us to save Michelle's life. With everything arranged and people hard at work clearing the runway, preparing the Learjet, and helping the family, it was time for me to head to the airport.

My son Derek would be my assistant and driver that day, but first he had to dig my car out of the snow. After that, he came back inside and stocked up our provisions; we headed out for the airport to help.

Very little snow and ice had been cleared from the city streets. We packed supplies of shovels and rock salt just in case. Skirting between stranded vehicles and snowdrifts on the road proved challenging.

Derek was familiar with traveling under adverse weather conditions, setting up concert gigs across the country. Growing up in Louisville, he knew all the secondary roads and what treeless streets to avoid where the snowstorm would have hit the hardest. We also had to avoid the locked-down interstate and found ourselves jackknifing our way through a maze of stranded cars.

As we drove, we intently listened to Mary Jeffries on the radio keeping everyone apprised of the Schmitt family's progress, as well as the airport clearing status.

3:15 p.m.—15 minutes to liftoff

As we approached the airfield, we saw the helicopter take off. This told us that the Schmitts were on board the jet and Jason Smith was ready to head out. We could also see the mounds of shoveled snow rimming the runway and the army of volunteers finishing the clearing.

Mary Jeffries gave her final report, saying that the jet was ready to fly out. We could hear the engines warming up as we parked the car. I got out and hurried over to the plane. Barbara was waiting at the bottom of the stairs for me to arrive. We shared a big hug.

"You made this happen, Sharon. And the girls and I will be forever grateful. God bless you!" Of course, on this day, the most important thing I could do after all I had worked toward for two years, the *only* thing I could do really, was to make the calls to get the ball rolling, give the family some hope, and then step back. Untold numbers of people made this happen. Some had been planning for this day for two years, helping me raise money, making donations, and praying. Some came into the picture just this day, at a time when there was nothing more I could do, and took over and saved the day. But, yes. This moment was the fulfillment of a mission, a calling I received two years earlier, the moment everything I had been through in my life had prepared me for. In that moment, all I could feel was anticipation and gratitude. So much had happened to get us to this point. But Michelle was a long way from saved. It was too early to celebrate.

Ed now came to the door, waved to me, and told me to come up, that the girls wanted to say hello. So I followed Barbara up the stairs. I particularly wanted to see Michelle, knowing what was in store for her.

Ashley was sitting a few seats down. She jumped up and ran to me, giving me a big hug. Then she stepped back and looked at me more closely. My pants were soaked from tromping through the snow to get to the plane.

I could see her concern. "I'm okay. How are you and your sister?"

Ashley smiled. "I'm fine, but Michelle looks scared."

I followed her back to where Barbara was holding Michelle on her lap. I squatted down to look her in the eyes. "Are you okay, dear?"

With her pippy in her mouth, she nodded her head tentatively.

"Just think of the airplane like Big Bird on Sesame Street flying you to get your new liver."

She smiled and said, "Big Bird," two beautiful words from a little child who up to that point had said nothing more to me than sounds that meant "yes" and "no."

"Yes. Just know that everybody at the hospital wants the best for you and just do as they say, and all this sickness will go away."

Michelle nodded again, and Barbara grasped my hand. I stood up and told all three of them, "I'll be here waiting for you to come home, and I want you to know that I love all of you very much." I looked at Barbara. "I'll call to check on you."

The copilot now stepped out of the cockpit and said they were ready to take off. I think turning away from Michelle and walking down the aisle to exit the plane was one of the hardest things I have ever done. As I passed Ed, we exchanged looks of concern. We were both worried about the surgery and its effect on his fragile daughter.

I guess I suffered from the same hidden fears about this surgery that Ed and Theresa had about Ashley's. I remembered him telling me what his wife had said to him: "She'll die for sure without the surgery." It felt as if Theresa was calling out and reassuring me from the other side.

I hurried down the airstair as the copilot, Jeff Bowman, secured the door. Derek and I stood back to allow the jet to taxi to the runway. The wings' tips skimmed the top of the snow mounds on both sides. The men who had worked for hours to clear the snow from the runway ran over to dust the snow off the wings.

The airplane now pulled onto the ice-covered runway, its engines building up thrust for the takeoff. This was the most precarious part of their journey to Omaha. Everybody was looking at one another, some with their heads bowed in prayer. The icy runway was not as long as the pilots would have liked and there was no margin for error to the left or right, either.

I had all the confidence in the world in our pilot, Jason Smith. I could hear some of the men say, "If anybody can make this work, it's Jason." But the pressure was on for him. He had to gain traction on an inch of ice and lift the jet into the air.

3:30 p.m.—January 17, 1994
The jet now pushed forward with the engines roaring louder and louder, gaining power and speed as it lumbered down the slippery runway and lifted off into the powder blue sky. A cheer went up from those gathered on the airfield. A few truckers beeped their horns.

I didn't meet Jim Patterson, the owner of the Pattco jet, until weeks after they flew Michelle to Omaha under those terrible weather conditions. By chance, he went to the barber across the hall from our salon. As he came out one day, I caught him in the hall and told him how much I appreciated what he did for Michelle.

He smiled and told me, "I was just glad we were the ones to get the call."

Airborne and on its way to Omaha was the inaugural "Angels Flight One." I had hopes there would be many more in the years to come, but today my thoughts were on this plane's sickly passenger, Michelle Schmitt. Getting her there in time for her surgery was only phase one of the mission.

We had done our job against incredible odds, and now it was time for the transplant surgeons in Omaha to do theirs. And across the country, as Michelle's family flew toward hope, another family was saying goodbye to their loved one. As I drove home with Derek, I couldn't help but feel a bit down, a natural emotion after going through a crisis. It was all out of my control now, and I had to rely on others, which wasn't easy for me.

On the television news that night, we heard that Jason had landed safely at Omaha's Eppley Field after fighting furious tail-winds over Nebraska. Michelle arrived at the hospital at 6:45 p.m. Central time, just fifteen minutes short of the deadline. Michelle was prepped for surgery, which began around midnight. She received her liver transplant without medical complications. Barbara called me afterward and said that she was doing fine. Ed reported to the press that Michelle was sitting up, wanting her bottle, and hungry.

The story was picked up by the newswire and highlighted in the national press.

Michelle went back to surgery the next day to receive her blood-lines, a routine procedure they performed a little early in her case due to her tiny veins collapsing. We followed the daily coverage, waiting for a definitive surgery report that she was on her way to a full recovery.

The day after that second surgery, I called Barbara in Omaha. She was upset and scared. Michelle was doing okay, but seeing her granddaughter on life support was harrowing for Barbara. Through-out this ordeal, Barbara would communicate Michelle's status to me, and I would update the media. Michelle's recovery was going to take months. They would be in Omaha for fifty-five days.

Both Barbara and I were swamped by media inquiries, which was taxing. This inspirational story was good for our community, however, and for the nation. It showed that miracles can and will happen when people from all walks of life unite to help others—in this case, to save a child's life.

While those involved patiently answered the questions posed to us by the media, it was always with an eye to Michelle's well-being. We were all concerned but hopeful, given her fragile condition, that she would have a full recovery.

The media's nationwide attention led to an inspiring and important connection. Geraldine Friesen, from Nebraska, read about Michelle's harrowing journey to receive her donor liver, and realized Michelle may very well have been the recipient of her own grandson's liver.

Brian Friesen, from Wichita, Kansas, was a beautiful seven-year-old boy who loved reading, music, his family, and Jesus. Perfectly healthy, on Saturday morning, January 15, 1994, Brian was playing with his younger brother Jesse when he screamed, feeling an unbearable pain in his head. Brian had suffered a brain aneurysm. He was rushed to the hospital, but there was nothing anyone could do. Brian died the next day, and his parents decided to donate his organs. Michelle did indeed receive his liver, but the privacy rules around donation prevented anyone from knowing where, or who, donations came from.

Brian's father, Orin Friesen, was a well-known bluegrass and country western radio disc jockey, and when his mother called with the story about Michelle, Orin reached out to his old friend, Coyote Calhoun, legendary Louisville disc jockey with WAMZ Radio. WAMZ was one of the many radio stations who broadcast the story, including the urgent need for volunteers to clear a place for the helicopter to land. He knew how to reach Michelle's father, Ed, and told him about Brian. Ed had always wanted to know where his older daughter Ashley's liver had come from, wanting to express his thanks to the family, but never found out. This was his chance to do so for Michelle, and he was not going to take no for an answer.

Ed made the call, and after a period of time checking and getting permissions, he got the confirmation he needed: Brian Friesen was indeed the donor of Michelle's liver. Coyote Calhoun connected Ed to the Friesen family, and late at night just a couple of days after the transplant, Ed called Orin and Bekki Friesen. This would be a huge moment of healing for both families, and the start of a life-long friendship.

Ed had given a lot of thought to the donating family and their loss, and was so pleased to connect with them. He asked them if they could use their son's name in their interviews with the press. They happily consented, and Ed gave me permission to mention Brian and the family in my press calls.

• • •

FOR WEEKS, AS the snow slowly melted, the Louisville community stayed close to their televisions and radios, waiting for updates from Omaha.

It felt good to answer my call and do God's work on this mission, a journey that began over twenty years before as I lay on that hospital gurney. I thanked God for allowing me to be of genuine service to someone I did not know. While this mission had its ups and downs, saving Michelle's life was the best reward any of us could ask for. I wondered what was next for me. Surely there would be more opportunities to help others.

I thanked God for Michelle's recovery and being given this chance at life and for all the volunteers who made this happen. All our promises were realized for the Schmitt family, but I might add they were for us as well. Blessings were bestowed on all of us through this ordeal. As the Bible says in Matthew 25:40, "Truly I say to you, to the extent that you did it to one of these brothers of Mine, *even* the least *of them*, you did it to Me.'"

Everyone in Louisville at that time will never forget the love this story brought out in us. We were all motivated to help this sickly child and her desperate family, and that feeling carried us forward—but we still had to get Michelle all the way home.

I feared that something might go wrong after her surgery. I tried to push these worries aside, but I was deeply concerned for this child's life. It was not over yet by any means; the first few weeks were the most critical.

I told everybody who asked to keep praying and keep a positive attitude, and Michelle would come back to us soon.

Three weeks after the surgery, Congressman Ron Mazzoli honored all the volunteers and acknowledged the selfless acts of the community of Louisville and Jefferson County by entering our story into the congressional record, on February 8, 1994. He quoted recent *Courier-Journal* articles in full and said,

> *I am immensely proud to represent such a dedicated and giving group of individuals. The work everyone put forth to give a little girl a chance for a full life was a labor of love and was evidence, once again, of the devotion and true charity of the people of Louisville and Jefferson County. The episode is a prime example of how noble and caring people are when called upon.*[6]

26

Welcome Home

JANUARY 17–MARCH 13, 1994

During Michelle's recovery time in Nebraska, the family sustained many highs and lows; I remained close to the Schmitts by phone. Barbara usually waited each day until she returned to her motel room before calling me.

Michelle came through the initial surgeries, and time was now on her side. She hung in there like a real trooper, as they say, but the recovery process was very hard for her, especially the drugs administered during and after surgery to keep her sedated.

Barbara and Ed worked as a tag team: one of them would stay at the hospital all night while the other got some sleep, and in the morning they would trade places so Michelle was never alone. Both took turns back at the motel caring for Ashley, who they brought in to the hospital to see her sister when she was allowed. Seeing Michelle's incremental recovery every day kept them going through the long days and nights.

Two weeks after her surgery, while I was talking to Barbara on the phone, she gave me the chance to speak to Michelle for the first time since her surgery. Back home, I would do all the talking; she would agree with an "uh huh," or disagree with a "huh uh," or nod or shake her head.

My heart was pounding as Barbara put the phone up to her ear. I asked, "Are you all right, dear?"

She answered with her usual, "Uh huh."

As I continued the conversation, I said, "I miss you very much, and I'm waiting for you to get well so you can come home to play with me!"

I could hear her and Ashley giggle on the other end and knew that she was aware it was me.

I added, "I've been watching you on television, and I can see that you're getting well. You have color in your cheeks and are putting on some weight."

Ashley took the phone from her and said, "She's going to be a fatty." They both giggled.

"I am going to let you go now, so you can rest and get well. I will call you tomorrow."

Michelle had spoken very little, rarely more than one word at a time, even though she was over three years old, but she listened to everything. This was a banner day for me when, to everyone's astonishment, Michelle said to me, "I love you." After all that she had gone through, those words took my breath away.

Barbara instantly grabbed the phone and said, "Did you hear what she said to you?"

I was so shocked I couldn't even respond. It was a moment that I will never forget and will always hold close to my heart. During this long ordeal, Barbara had asked many times, "How can we ever repay you?" Well, in those three words, Michelle paid me in full.

I never wanted anything for doing what I did, nor did any of the other Angels, Inc. members, or any of the thousands of contributors and volunteers. I only wanted Michelle and Ashley to know that I cared, that the world cared, and especially that God cared about their well-being. So, as I put down the phone that day, it also made me reflect on all the people in my early years who had reached out and selflessly helped me.

People who have had near-death experiences say that it's not their accomplishments or possessions that pass in review but the love they've shared with others. That day, I came to understand the truth of that sentiment more than ever.

As time went on, Michelle began getting better day by day, and the worst was truly over. Calls about her progress and the background of her struggles came in from all over the country. Within the first two weeks, I had given about twenty interviews for television and radio news outlets and publications.

While the Schmitts were tending to Michelle in Omaha, and after getting regular reports on her recovery, I began putting together a "Welcome Home" gathering at the airport. This would be Michelle's first public appearance. Many people who had worked hard to make this happen wanted to come and show their support for her recovery.

Most volunteers and the town's citizens had never seen Michelle, except her picture on the donation jars everywhere. However, even after two months of recovery, she would still be too frail for anything but a wave as she was carried down the airstair. We had something else planned for much later—a much larger celebration.

While we would encourage people to show up at the airport on Michelle's arrival, the broader program would have to wait because her viral resistance would be so low her first few months home. It would take time for the medication to build up her immunity, and there were risks for her being out in public.

This lengthy recovery time also gave me more time, with Derek's help, to create a unique and uplifting thank-you program, with musical and celebrity guests. There were literally hundreds of volunteers who needed to be acknowledged, though few would have asked for it. Still, Ed and I wanted to include as many as we could.

Given the national media coverage, we were getting inquiries from Hollywood. We had interviews and articles in publications such as *Woman's Day* magazine and *Woman's World* and television interviews on *A Current Affair* and *Inside Edition*. Ed had asked that I handle these inquiries. So we decided on one and signed with them.

While the articles, especially the day-to-day local newspaper and television coverage, would help with donations, more financial influx was needed for Michelle's recovery and digging the family out of their massive medical debt.

In addition to insurance deductibles to meet, there would also be follow-up medical checkups at the hospital in Omaha, Nebraska, and the flights to and from the hospital, which would not be covered by insurance.

Perhaps all this attention would not only increase donations, but inspire other communities to seek out families in similar need and help them. As our Angel slogan says, "*With God, all things are possible.*" If we were able to establish regular donations, Angels, Inc. could move on to help more children in this situation.

While discussions with national publications continued, I was busy planning our production that grew more expansive with every day. At first, I thought it would be just a small get-together to honor our volunteers and workers. But, as Michelle's story made the media rounds, we got inquiries about a televised event.

We decided to include an awards ceremony to honor those who were with us from the start, like our hairdressers at the first hair-a-thon. Then there were all the companies and banks who gave huge donations, deferred payments, or forgave debt. I wanted everyone to know about them.

We wanted to include the workers who showed up in arctic weather and cleared tons of snow off the church parking lot and the Pattco jet's runway. Television news crews had filmed that heroic effort. The world needed to know what could be done under severe conditions when people unite for a worthy cause.

I named our show "Angel Day USA." We also added a special award to be called "The Angels Choice Award." The Angels board of directors would choose its recipient from the people or groups we felt most deserved the recognition.

For the Special Award trophy, I went to Barney Bright, a world-renowned Louisville Artist. I visited him at his studio and talked about our mission and Angels, Inc. He came up with the idea of an angel holding a child as the sculpture. The sculpture, finished, stands about fifteen inches high.

Bright donated the sculpture to Angels, Inc. for the award. I was amazed when I first saw the sculpture. I could only think that it was divinely inspired. Later, he used the mold to cast a few more for special clients.

Then after months in Omaha, it was time for Michelle's return to Louisville. I was so excited to see her again. The family would have liked a low-key airport arrival, but the media got wind of her flight, and we were forced to stage a citizen's welcome home.

I went to the airport to wait for the flight to come in while the mayor's office had the police put up barricades to keep the press and local well-wishers at a discrete distance. I gave the press a briefing as the plane approached for its landing.

"We'd like to keep this as a family event, so there won't be interviews with the Schmitts today. I will now take some questions and try to answer them." I understood that reporters would be rushing to post their stories for their morning papers, here and nationwide.

Ed had briefed me as to his daughter's condition and the time needed for her recovery. I told the press that she would be confined to her home for three to five months, with periodic checkups with her doctors in Omaha. She was well, and the surgery was a complete success.

When Michelle and her family came through the doors, there was a rousing cheer from everybody gathered there. Ed and Barbara had tears in their eyes. Michelle walked along, swinging her arm in a cute, sassy way as cameras flashed, a stylish fascinator hat perched on her head for her return to the Derby city. She spotted me and immediately rushed over and gave me a big hug.

The Schmitt family returns from Michelle's life-saving liver transplant. Front row from left: Ashley Schmitt, cousin Matthew Stewart, Michelle Schmitt, grandfather Ed Schmitt. Rear: father Ed Schmitt. Photo originally published in the Louisville Courier-Journal, March 13, 1994. Photo credit: ©Christina Freitag 1994

Given Michelle's delicate condition, Barbara kept her at a distance from the press and the crowd, and after posing for a few long-distance photos, we hustled the family to our car and police escort. I rode with them to their home, and Michelle sat on my lap the whole way. At one point, I whispered in her ear, "I love you."

"I love you," she said with a smile.

Barbara just shook her head. After Michelle's surgery she roused quickly, asking for her favorite food and drink, more talkative than she had ever been—a sign she was feeling so much better.

• • •

AFTER OUR EXTENDED reunion, I went back to work preparing for the award ceremony, about three months away, which would give Michelle's immune system time to strengthen.

Thankfully, I had Derek's help arranging the musical side of the event. He and his father were gathering musicians to play the program, so we quickly secured a location and fixed the date. Fortunately, a lot of people volunteered their services, from caterers to security people.

I had many speeches to write, acknowledging every individual and group who had aided our mission. I wanted to make all of them feel special and gave much loving care to the wording for each of their salutes. This was about people coming together to help those in need, especially children and their families.

This event would be Michelle's first public appearance since her recuperation from the transplant. Without putting too much stress on her, we wanted everyone who had worked so hard for her to see the success of her liver transplant.

27

Brian's Gift

JUNE 25, 1994

Finally, the weekend for our celebration arrived. The KFC Corporation graciously flew Brian Friesen's family to Louisville to meet the Schmitts and attend the ceremony. The Schmitts met the Friesen family at the airport without the attention of the media, and the two families quietly slipped out to the Schmitt home to share a meal and spend several hours getting to know each other. I could only imagine what it must have been like for Bekki Friesen to hold Michelle, knowing her son's liver gave this sweet little girl new life.

The Friesen family at the Schmitt home. Left to right, Ed Schmitt, Ashley Schmitt, Michelle Schmitt, Bekki Friesen, Jesse Friesen, and Orin Friesen.
Photo courtesy of the Friesen family.

The Brown Hotel provided the Friesens with a free room and meals. With the Friesens in town and settled, the Schmitt family ready to go, and everyone in place, it looked like the program was going ahead full speed. I just had to pull off my part of the program without crying through the whole production.

I went to the Kentucky Center for the Arts for early rehearsals on the day of our "Angel Day USA" event. We all met on the stage and talked through the program. Everyone knew their role and was excited.

Not long before the evening was to begin, the Friesen and Schmitt families arrived backstage as the seats in the auditorium began to fill up. Even though Michelle and Ashley seemed to be looking forward to it, the event was certainly going to go past their usual bedtime, and they had enjoyed a very busy day already. I hoped they would not be too tired to enjoy themselves.

When it was almost time for me to go onstage, I suddenly had no idea what I was going to say. I knew the order of presentations and I had prepared acknowledgments for everyone, but in that moment, my mind went blank, and I froze.

Then, the lights took us to darkness, and the soft, delicate tones of a harpist opened the show, followed by performances from more special guests. The energy in the theater was exhilarating, but I couldn't move.

As I watched this opening musical program from backstage, my stage appearance minutes away, Eddie Humphries gently touched my shoulder and asked, "Could you use a prayer about now?" I had known Eddie for years. He was in my first husband's band, Soul, Inc. Eddie was the friend who had first suggested I visit Southeast Christian Church and was also playing in the production, the next to go on.

"Yes!" I said, turning to Eddie. His prayer reminded me to call upon God's Holy Spirit for my inspiration. It was like God tapping me on the shoulder and reminding me, "Fear not, for I am with you always."

John Tong, treasured Louisville sportscaster, was our master of ceremonies. He spoke of Angels, Inc., who had first rallied Louisville's support for Michelle and her family. Then he introduced me as president and founder of the organization.

The audience's applause bolstered my courage. I started by telling the story of how reading Jim Adams' article in the *Courier-Journal* newspaper about the Schmitt family's struggle was my inspiration. I then spoke about the people who came forward for two years to help us raise over $50,000 for the family.

I presented each person and group I spoke about with an Angel certificate to recognize their gracious work to save a child's life. This lineup included all the corporations, the social clubs, hospitals, churches throughout the Louisville community, and my beloved hair-a-thon team.

As I told about the day of the flight, I gave certificates to the people who dug out the plane, the pilots who flew the Schmitt family to Omaha, WHAS Radio, and all of the first responders and medical team who could attend.

The KFC Corporation received a certificate and also sent us two wonderful speakers: Rick Laughlin, whose jet was on standby the whole time, and his son Nicholas, who urged everyone to sign up to become organ donors.

I concluded and talked about Michelle and the severity of her condition. I reminded the audience that our story turned into a great success.

A dim blue spotlight in the center of the stage slowly brightened a table with the satin-cloth-veiled Angel art piece sculpted by Barney Bright.

The sculpture designed and cast by Barney Bright.

I brought Michelle and her family onto the stage, who stood together on one side of the table. For the first time that evening, the public could witness the extraordinary difference the transplant surgery had on this child. With rosy cheeks and added weight, Michelle captivated the audience with her smile.

I next introduced the Friesens, and told the audience about the tragic loss of their son Brian at age seven, and their decision to share his organs to help other children. I lauded their courage in the midst of such a tragedy. Needless to say, the Angel's Choice Award went to the Friesens, awarded by Michelle herself with a hug and a kiss to Bekki Friesen, Brian's mother.

Bekki and Orin Friesen were captivated by the beauty of the angel sculpture, but also the meaning it had for them and their beloved Brian.

Following that divine moment, a gospel choir of forty-two children sang their hearts out. People were now out of their seats, clapping their hands. It was an absolutely wonderful scene. You could almost see the glowing rays of God's Holy Spirit touching everybody gathered there.

The program closed with a song. While the curtain closed, we could hear the singing and clapping dissolve into lively chatter from the audience.

After several moments, I was able to reach my own family, who had been so instrumental, not just this night, but throughout the past two years. I was heartened to find my biological mother, Anna, whom I had not seen in many years, waiting to see me. In spite of our difficult and painful relationship, it was her life in ministry that I had eventually followed.

It was a memorable night for all of us, and the blessings were abundant. I ultimately found Michelle, and we hugged as I told her how wonderful she was onstage. She showed off her pretty ruffled dress. I was so proud of her and her big sister, Ashley.

The following day I drove to the Schmitts for Sunday brunch and to spend time with the Friesens. I arrived early to help Barbara in the kitchen, but she had everything already completed and waiting.

While waiting for the Friesens, I visited the girls and played with them until our guests arrived. Then, when the doorbell rang, we all ran downstairs to greet them with hugs.

They had brought the angel art piece with them and placed it on the fireplace mantel for all of us to see. We oohed and ahhed at this magnificent artwork, so special to the family.

They told us in more detail about Brian, expressing their feelings in depth. Brian was only seven years old when he suddenly suffered an aneurysm that took his precious life. He had told his teacher and other friends that he wanted to be a minister when he grew up. Brian was a good student and well liked, and it seemed as if everyone noticed that he had a special spiritual connection.

Orin Friesen, a disc jockey at KFDI radio station in Wichita, Kansas, shared his wonderful memories of Brian, and we marveled again at the miraculous way God used his radio connections to unite these two families.

Bekki told me that she had often thought about angels, long before Brian's death. Thus, the sculpture's details of the child embraced by the angel had a very peaceful meaning for them. I was very proud to have had Barney Bright's sculpture as our special award at the event. His art piece went to a home with even greater appreciation than any artist could hope for.

Jesse Friesen, Brian's younger brother, missed him very much. He was very young to have sustained the loss of a sibling, and not just an older brother but a best friend. Brian's maternal grandmother, Lindsay Gardner, was also present.

Seeing these two families together celebrating the continuity of life was both gratifying and humbling; for all that we had done to get to this point, no one had sacrificed more than the Friesens. I was so glad God arranged for these two families to meet, in spite of the obstacles the transplant process has in place to protect everyone's privacy. There was no doubt, this was all part of a larger plan, and I played just a small part in it.

Brunch was served, and we shared food, stories, and heartfelt laughter while watching Jesse and the girls play together and do funny things to entertain us. This gentle goodbye away from the cameras and crowds of well-wishers was just what these two families needed, still traumatized by all they had been through the past six months.

As it turned out, I needed this moment, too, to be in the room where my relationship with the Schmitts started over two years earlier, and to start the process of letting go so they could get on with finding their "new normal."

28

Moving On

1994–PRESENT

Moving on from a mission that had consumed me for so long was harder than I thought it would be, but the Schmitts were gracious enough to include me in the girls' lives for many years. They also maintained contact with the Friesens. Over the years, Michelle and Ashley would visit the Friesen family multiple times, and developed a wonderful connection with them and their children.

Watching Ashley and Michelle grow was always pure joy. Throughout those years of struggle, Barbara dressed them to perfection in dresses with bows in their hair. They were so dainty and tiny and the best-behaved children you could ever imagine. At that time, their lives revolved a lot around their conditions and the extra precautions their father had to take. They were raised in

The Schmitt girls at dinner with Jesse Friesen. Left to right, Michelle Schmitt, Jesse Friesen, and Ashley Schmitt. Photo courtesy of the Friesen family.

church and had good values from their grandparents and father; you couldn't find nicer people.

I returned to my regular routine as a hair designer. Barbara regularly brought the girls to the salon. I would take time to do their hair, and later visit with them at home. Like always, we would play games together.

After her surgery, Michelle quickly started to thrive. She was so outgoing and spunky and made us all laugh at every turn. Michelle was rapidly adjusting to life as a healthy little girl, just as Ashley had done after her own transplant surgery. All the things Michelle once couldn't do, she was trying all at once. It was heartwarming to watch her explore her new world and know she was so happy with her newfound agility.

Michelle and Ashley were about as opposite as two sisters could be. Michelle was a little live wire, always waiting for something to laugh at, very engaging and active. Ashley was quiet and observant, but as she grew older, I watched her start to relax and laugh with us. Soon it was time for Ashley to start school, and I knew she would excel in her studies. I guess I bonded a little more with her from our history together and because she was a little older.

I was blessed to watch them grow up and mature and develop their own individuality. Throughout the years, they developed just like any other children, even though they had more health issues to face. It seemed like their ongoing health issues deepened them and made them more mature as they entered their teenage years. While they enjoyed life, getting caught up in this or that craze, at times I could almost see their souls shining through their eyes. Interacting with them deepened my spiritual commitment.

The girls continued to come to visit me at the salon, even after Barbara passed away. At first, their grandfather would bring them and wait patiently for his beautiful granddaughters' visit to end. One day when they came to my salon alone, I asked them where their grandpa was. They both yelled out at the same time, "Ashley got her driver's license!"

This news took me by surprise. Because of their health issues and stringent medication regimens, they were very small for their age. At age sixteen, Ashley could almost pass as a nine-year-old. This rite of passage snapped me out of the past and into the girls' present. They were growing up quickly! However, it took me awhile to wrap my head around it.

Then, only a few visits later, they returned just as excited, but Michelle's voice drowned out Ashley's this time. "We're getting growth treatments!"

I was a bit confused. "What are growth treatments?" I had no idea there was such a thing. At that moment, Michelle quickly looked to her big sister to bail her out. She explained that the treatment was a series of hormone shots that would help them catch up in their physical development.

Then Michelle giggled, "What if we become as big as giants?"

Ashley joined in on the frivolity, "Like Paul Bunyan!"

I was so glad for them, and their humor sent an electric volt of joy to my heart.

Eventually, I relocated my salon closer to my home, and the girls stopped visiting. Life went on and we lost contact until years later.

The Spirit of God touched this story from beginning to end. Our purpose was to follow God's will to provide for and protect the girls, and we did. Afterward, we all went on with our lives. This is just what is supposed to happen. Yet, the story didn't end there for any of us.

The Schmitt girls moved on to lead regular lives, learning life lessons, suffering setbacks, working hard for the life they wanted, and enjoying all the moments we worked so hard for them to have. This was all we wanted for them, and it was extremely gratifying to see.

• • •

THE CITY OF Louisville never lost a beat. I will never forget what a city, *this* city, accomplished together, out of love and compassion for a little girl they had never met. Almost thirty years later, Louisville would unite again in a very different way, to fight for justice for another beautiful girl most had never met but the entire world would soon come to care about, Breonna Taylor. For all of this city's problems, these two dramatically different situations show that the people of Louisville have a heart full of love for each other, regardless of race or religion. This is what it's all about. It's what I am most proud of.

• • •

I MOVED ON too. I resumed my work styling hair, but the work I had hoped would continue with Angels, Inc., helping other children in need, ended quickly. I never forgot the lessons I learned about myself, about saying yes when God calls, and about what he can do with the little we have to give him.

In the decades that followed, I also enjoyed all the moments life has given me and experienced many highs and lows, downturns in health and fortune, and upturns in friendship and opportunity. Now well into my senior years, few people know me by this extraordinary story. I am just an ordinary grandma, friend, mom, and, once upon a time, an angel in my own small way to a little girl and her family, who in turn became an angel to me, knocking down decades of walls I had built to keep my heart from being hurt again, and teaching me that everything I had experienced in my broken life was being used for good. As I said at the beginning, not a single tear was wasted.

May 9, 2021

I think it was a Sunday morning. I never watch the news on Sunday morning, but this morning, for some reason, I did.

Ashley's face was on the news. Why? My heart jumped into my throat as I turned up the volume on the television and leaned in. Michelle was gone. Michelle was gone, and I didn't understand what had happened.

Later that week I would pull myself together and attend the funeral to pay my respects.

The funeral was held in a metal building, a multipurpose room with concrete floors and pews sitting in order, facing a pulpit set up for the service. Surprisingly, I didn't recognize anyone and sat in the back. Then, Ashley and her dad appeared. As I saw Ed, I instinctively reached out to comfort him. His head dropped to his chest and his eyes filled with tears. I was surprised that he would release his grief with me in this way; we didn't know each other very well at all, despite all we had been through together. I used a quiet, calming voice to try to comfort him.

We talked a little about the room, and I told him it was perfect.

"Michelle would have loved it," I told him. "It was *her.*" He smiled and nodded at this perspective, then walked to the front to take his seat.

The service was wonderful and sweet. I could feel Michelle's presence as I watched Ashley, but I could see she was reeling from the loss. For all these two had been through, all the times in the past that death had nearly separated them, it was still a shock to lose her little sister.

To all of us who loved her, Michelle's sudden passing on May 7, 2021, at age thirty-one was a great loss. But for her best friend Crystal; her sister Ashley; Michelle's husband David; and her father Ed, each felt as if they had lost a part of their soul at that moment. Her father was completely heartbroken, as death had followed him throughout his adult years. The grief this man endured was overwhelming.

Michelle left us after living a full, rich life—exactly what we all wanted for her—and along the way she enriched everyone around her. I only wish she could have had many more years.

• • •

THESE WERE SOME of the countless memories that this journey bestowed on me, helping me to reconcile some of my own childhood trauma, to see purpose in all of the dysfunction and rejection I had lived through. Whatever passion I brought to this impossible mission was forged under the heavy hammer of my past. I was glad to be there when Michelle needed me the most, and in a roundabout way, I came to need her and this experience just as much.

After that time, my life went back to where it was before that fateful day at my kitchen table. Still, our paths would cross again in a most unusual way, many years later. It seemed God was not finished with this miracle just yet.

Epilogue

In so many ways, this incredible account continues to grow and be an inspiration, now decades later. Following are updates on a few of the people you have come to care about in the story:

- The Friesen Family
- A Stunning Misdiagnosis
- Crystal Olafson
- Michelle Schmitt (and spouse, David Cobble)
- Ashley Schmitt
- Ed Schmitt
- Sharon Stevens
- The Extraordinary Origin of the Movie

THE FRIESEN FAMILY

Brian Friesen was the seven-year-old boy whose brain aneurysm took his beautiful life on January 16, 1994, and whose liver was successfully donated to Michelle. His last gift, though, was received in the days and weeks following his funeral, something extraordinary and intensely comforting to his family, and through their testimony, to all of us.

As early as age five, Brian became more and more interested in the subject of God, angels, and heaven, asking deep questions far beyond his years. When asked what he wanted to be when he grew up, the handsome then-six-year-old child immediately responded he wanted to be a pastor.

No one really knows when he started writing and drawing notes to his family and hiding them around the house, but it couldn't have been long before that terrible Saturday morning.

Shortly after the funeral Brian's mom, dad, and brother began finding them. The first note they found read, "I love you all and Jesus does, too. Hope you have a good time. Brian."

Brian Friesen. Photo courtesy of the Friesen family.

After they found a second note, they began to anticipate when they might discover another. They found another, then another, each one delivering comfort and joy to the grief-stricken family.

Roughly six weeks after Brian's death, Orin and Bekki decided to take Jesse and get away for a while. As Orin pulled his suitcase out to pack, he found a large, colorful drawing that Brian had made and hidden inside this piece of luggage. Orin said, "It was the most amazing picture. There were trees and a little kid and a mound with a cross on it—a grave." When asked by a writer for a church publication if he thought Brian somehow suspected he was going to die, he responded, "I don't know how he could have, but those notes are so comforting to us. We know that Brian is with Jesus and that's the greatest comfort of all."

While Michelle was on her way to Omaha to receive Brian's liver, other organ recipients in multiple states were also being prepped to receive Brian's heart, both of his kidneys, and his corneas. One

The drawing Brian Friesen hid in his parents' suitcase, along with two of the love notes he hid around their home. Photo courtesy of the Friesen family.

of Brian's kidneys went to a man in Wichita, and the other one to another man in the Midwest. His heart went to a five-year-old girl named Rachel, somewhere on the East Coast. The Friesens received letters from Rachel's mother and from both kidney recipients, delivered anonymously through the organ donation process.

Three years after Brian's passing, the Friesens added a daughter, Annie, to their family, who is a talented artist, drawn to outdoor studies and work. Annie and Jesse have an older sibling, Josh, who is an associate athletics director and coach at a private college prep school in Texas. As of this printing, Orin and Bekki will have been married over forty years.

Orin continued his work as a disc jockey and "singing cowboy," still performing today in his late seventies. His deep roots in bluegrass also tied him to Kentucky and the Louisville area, one of the reasons he was able to find a way to connect with the Schmitt family. The Friesens' son, Jesse, followed in his musical footsteps as a performing artist and sound engineer, and now is back in Kansas playing with his dad in the Diamond W Wranglers, a popular country-western band.

So far, the Friesens have found thirteen notes, the most recent found years after Brian's passing, and wonder if still more are hidden, waiting to be discovered just when they need them the most. Bekki has carefully kept each note in an album.

A STUNNING MISDIAGNOSIS

Sometime in the early 2000s, Michelle and Ashley went through a series of tests, including a "targeted gene panel." Doctors were hoping to solve the mystery of how these two sisters ended up with the same rare non-hereditary disease.

All their lives, medical professionals had believed they both suffered from biliary atresia, a condition that strikes roughly one in every 15,000 people. The odds that two people in the same household would fall victim to this same rare condition were astronomically low, and this is why Ed and Theresa were given the all-clear to have more children after Ashley was born.

More than a decade after their respective liver transplants, DNA testing revealed a completely different diagnosis. Both Ashley and Michelle learned they had Byler's syndrome, or Byler disease, rather than biliary atresia. According to the University of Pittsburgh Medical Center, Byler disease is extremely rare, occurring only in about 1 in 50,000 to 1 in 100,000 babies, and "can look similar to biliary atresia."[7] With either diagnosis, a liver transplant would still likely have been the best treatment at the time.

However, there is a huge difference between the two diagnoses. Biliary atresia is not hereditary, but Byler disease is, in fact, a hereditary disease. Both parents must carry the recessive gene, and if they do, their offspring each have a 25 percent chance of inheriting some form of the disease. In all probability, both Ed and Theresa carried this recessive gene.

Byler disease was actually discovered about thirty years before the Schmitt sisters were born, but little was known about it, and presumably the tests for it were still relatively unknown back in the dawn of the Internet age. *Had Ashley been identified as having this disease, her parents would likely have decided not to have any more children.*

Think about this for a moment. Michelle would probably never have been born, nor would Ashley have had any other siblings, no one to grow up with who understood what she was going through. There would be no "Snowbaby," no heroic community rally to save her life, and Brian Friesen's liver may not have been a match for any other child that devastating January in 1994.

As difficult as the road has been for the Schmitt family, as crushing as Michelle's passing has been for her husband, family, and friends, no one would say it wasn't worth every second to have her in their lives. This missed diagnosis was perhaps the best thing that could have happened. Michelle Schmitt Cobble made an indelible impact on the world and in countless lives, including Sharon, and most especially, her own beloved family.

So, it seems, God's fingerprints can be seen in everything—most especially in our mistakes, our missed opportunities, our worst days—and he will bring it all together for good.

"And we know that God causes all things to work together for good to those who love God, to those who are called according to His purpose." Romans 8:28

So much more is known today about the various forms of liver disease than when the Schmitt sisters were born, including different treatment options, but there is still much to be learned. In 2002, a support organization was formed to provide advocacy, resources, and empowerment for patients with any of the six forms of inherited liver disease known as "Progressive Familial Intrahepatic Cholestasis" (PFIC), which includes Byler disease. A link to this organization is on the resource page.

CRYSTAL OLAFSON

Throughout Michelle's and Ashley's lives, even though health crises continued to give them setbacks, they shared many friends and activities. At age seven, Michelle met and formed a sweet friendship with one special girl, Crystal Olafson, who eventually would become close to Ashley as well. They loved Disney, so they made a point to go to the movies together every time another animated Disney movie was released. Crystal bonded with them as they grew up together. She went through so much with Ashley and Michelle, everyone thought of her as if she were their sister. What happened next would draw them closer still.

Crystal had always said, half joking, "If you need a kidney, I've got two!" Of course, she would have to be a perfect match for that to happen. Almost everyone can become a living kidney donor, since we have two kidneys but only need one working kidney. In order for a donor kidney to be a match for the recipient, the donor's blood goes through a testing process. The closer the match, the more likely the transplant will be successful, and the longer the kidney will last. A closely matched kidney could last more than forty years, or the rest of the recipient's natural life.

At one point, Ashley once again faced a health crisis, not uncommon with liver transplant recipients. She would need a kidney transplant, and Crystal immediately volunteered to be tested. The same week they were supposed to find out if Crystal was a match, Ashley received the good news that a kidney match was found from a person who had passed away. On June 4, 2011, Ashley received a kidney transplant.

Later that year, the girls were once again visiting the Friesens in Kansas when Michelle suddenly became very ill and was rushed to the hospital. Suffering from acute kidney failure, Michelle would also need a kidney transplant, as soon as possible. She was put on a medical flight back to Louisville, and Crystal once again was tested to see if she could donate her kidney. Doctors were astounded to find that Crystal's kidney compatibility was the closest they had seen from a non-relative; it was as if Crystal was actually Michelle's biological sister. After spending so much time together as best friends, Crystal would graciously give Michelle one of her kidneys.

Imagine the astonishment and joy in learning that such a perfect match was found in your best friend!

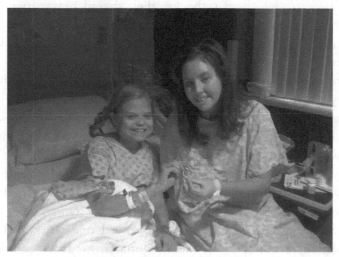

Crystal visits Michelle for the first time following the kidney transplant.
Photo courtesy of Sharon VanArsdale.

Donors in this case always have a longer and more difficult recovery period. Two days after the transplant, Crystal was able to sit up and spend some time in the chair beside her hospital bed. She soon made her way across the hall to Michelle's room, where she found her sitting up and enjoying a hamburger. Crystal's mother captured the moment.

For years all three young women served as advocates for various transplant programs, always there to help others, tirelessly participating in fundraisers and encouraging others to sign up to be organ donors.

Crystal's kidney donation gave Michelle nine and a half more healthy years. When Michelle began experiencing symptoms, she texted Ashley and Crystal throughout the day. When she was taken to the hospital, Crystal was one of Ashley's first calls, and she was with Ashley, David, and Ed during Michelle's last few moments.

Since then, Crystal and Ashley have worked through their grief together, conquering the many difficult moments we face after losing someone who has been a part of us all our lives. Crystal, now married with a child of her own, wrote:

"My entire life I have been a 'planner person.' Whether it be a calendar on a wall, an agenda, or a super expensive page-by-page customized planner. Each month when I turn to the next page I use a paper clip to pin back the lasts month's pages—all of these pages that Michelle never existed in. Turning to a new page, a blank one, letting time move on without her. Letting life go forward without her. But I did it, I did turn those pages back and clip them away again. I did it because I can't stop it from being July any more than I can stop Michelle from being gone.

For the rest of my life I will daydream about her being here, about what she'd say, about her laugh. Man do I miss that chuckle. It makes me chuckle just thinking about it. But most importantly, every month I'll keep turning the pages and clipping back the old ones, tucking them away safely and securely. Then I'll keep moving forward because Michelle would have wanted Ashley and me to do that! So we will, together, best friends . . . until we are eighty-something and we do something crazy that lands us up there with her."

MICHELLE SCHMITT: 1990-2021

Michelle graduated from Seneca High School, Louisville, in 2009, and received her BA in Psychology from Spalding University in 2013. She worked at Norton Hospital's Novak Center for Children's Health, where she occasionally worked with some of the pediatricians she and Ashley used to see as children. Michelle was able to help children with life-threatening illnesses, later commenting in an interview, "I know what some of the kids are going through. I definitely know I'm here for a reason."

She met her future husband, David, in a Kroger grocery checkout line. After a year or so of these frequent encounters, Michelle finally asked David if he wanted to "hang out." David later said, "I remember being so nervous when I met her family for the first time! I was trying to impress her dad and papaw and really, I was terrified. I appreciated Crystal's jokes and efforts to break the awkwardness. That ended up being the same night my grandmother passed away. I called Michelle and told her the news and she rushed over to be with me. She met my entire family at the funeral and stayed with me the whole day. After feeling her caring and compassion in such a tough situation, I knew she was the one for me.

"After telling her father and papaw how much I loved her and getting their blessing (it felt like a scene from *The Godfather*!), I was ready to ask her to be my wife. I finally worked up the nerve to ask her at the 2014 Louisville Kidney Walk. Everyone knew what was about to happen except Michelle. Finally, I told her how I felt, got on one knee, and asked her to marry me. She started crying and just nodded her head yes. There was a DJ there and he asked, 'Uh . . . did she say yes?' Then with tears and excitement she screamed YES!! I had never been happier than I was in that moment. I was so excited to spend the rest of our lives together."

After their wedding on May 16, 2015, the two decided to start a family of the furry variety. Since Michelle could not have children, the two adopted "Chewie," a Shih Tzu puppy, and "Reesie," a Cavalier mix. They attended Northeast Christian Church and enjoyed building their world together, eyes wide open about the fragility of life.

Michelle and David Cobble on their wedding day. Photo courtesy of Ashley Schmitt.

As the media had been doing on milestone dates throughout the years, on January 17, 2019, the *Courier-Journal* ran a story on the twenty-fifth anniversary of the snowstorm that paralyzed the state, focusing most of the article on the miraculous rescue of the little girl who had come to be known as "The Louisville Snowbaby." They interviewed Michelle, writing that "she knew she had God, her family and friends, donor Brian, and the hundreds of people in Louisville who didn't know her but helped anyway, to thank for her life." Michelle said, "It was a miracle. Nobody is wrong to call me that, because I am. And I'm not the only miracle that's running around out there. I am proof that everyone can get along and come together to help someone."[8]

May 2021

On Wednesday morning, May 5, 2021, after David had already left for work, Michelle got ready and took the dogs for a walk before she headed out to her job, just as she had done almost every morning. During the walk, she felt as if she might pass out and started experiencing severe abdominal pain. She texted Ashley and Crystal. *Should I go to the hospital?* she worried. With great difficulty, she was able to get back home and into bed. Just a little over a year since the COVID pandemic began, both she and Ashley learned to take every symptom seriously, but going to the hospital in the age of COVID was risky, also.

One of the more common complications liver transplant recipients might experience is cirrhosis of the liver, a treatable condition that may first be noticeable when fluid begins to accumulate in a person's abdomen. Michelle had been diagnosed with this complication and had been treating it since 2015. When she noticed fluid around her stomach, she thought it was a sign of cirrhosis—serious, but not an emergency situation. That night, however, the pain had become unbearable, and David called 911. Ashley rushed over, and spoke to her before the ambulance took her to the emergency room. "Please take care of Chewie and Reesie," Michelle asked her sister, her mind racing as David prepared to follow the squad to the hospital.

Late that night, after a battery of tests, Michelle texted: "I am bleeding somewhere internally. They are talking about possible surgery or a drainage procedure." She had already been given two bags of blood and her levels were lower than they were when she entered the hospital. She called each of her loved ones, assuring them she would call back if and when the doctors decided to operate. Toward the end of her call with Ashley, Michelle's voice changed suddenly, just before the call dropped. That was the last call Michelle would make.

Ashley's phone rang shortly after; the hospital needed permission to rush her back to surgery. Her blood pressure had bottomed out, causing her to lose consciousness. Ashley and Ed sped to the hospital. Almost immediately, prayers were going out for Michelle as word spread. Over the next hour or so, surgeons worked furiously to find the source of the bleeding and stop it.

Unsuccessful, the surgical team packed her stomach to stem the bleeding and brought her to the transplant ICU to rest while they strategized about what to try next, and when. The family was allowed to wait by her bedside, talk to her, and hold her hands. She was unconscious, hooked up to monitors and lines, with a constant stream of attendants replacing IV bags of platelets, blood, and fluid, working to raise her body temperature, and tracking her vitals.

No one knew if Michelle was aware they were there or not. Before they were sent back out to the waiting room, David, Ed, Crystal, and Ashley said their goodbyes—just in case she could hear them, and in the event they never got another chance. Sometime well after midnight, Michelle was taken back for a radiology procedure.

Finally after working feverishly for hours, the medical team spotted the aneurysm in her stomach and worked to determine how, or if, they were going to be able to clip and remove it. The radiologist came out to give the family the report, advising them to go home and get a couple hours' sleep.

The family did go home, but there was little sleep to be had. Ashley recalls: "I remember feeding our dog Winter that morning, and sitting in the living room with Dad. I started crying and told him I didn't think she was going to make it."

Just a couple of hours after they got home, the doctor called Ashley, asking for them to come in. David, Ashley, and Ed headed to the hospital, and Ashley called Crystal to come in. Ashley recalls: "We got down to the hospital and the doctor came in to speak with us. He said they had performed some neuro tests and they showed she had no brain activity. Her organs were all shutting down."

The family gathered together, and made the decision to take Michelle off of life support. Ashley remembers the respect and dignity of the moment: "The doctor who came in to unhook her was so kind. He talked to Michelle and told her everything he was going to do before he did it. All of us were standing around her, holding her hand or touching a part of her while she took her last breaths."

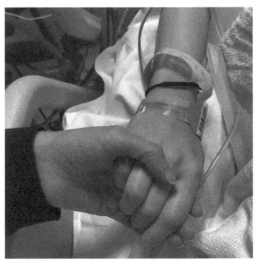

Ashley holding Michelle's hand. Photo courtesy Crystal Olafson

The medical team left the room to give the family privacy. Just a few minutes later, at 11:20 a.m., Michelle passed away.

• • •

MICHELLE WAS THIRTY-ONE when she died from a stomach aneurysm that had hemorrhaged. There were several moments when she was surrounded by her loved ones as they took the time to talk to her, say their goodbyes, and express their love, wondering if she could hear them and understand. Ironically, almost fifty years earlier, Sharon was about thirty when she was in a hospital room, dying from an internal hemorrhage, surrounded by a medical team, working feverishly to save her. Sharon's experience that day of being able to look down, to hear and see everyone, may provide a comforting answer to that question, and others. Though it does not diminish the heaviness of the loss, it may be comforting to think that Michelle would have been at peace during those final moments, able to both see and hear her loved ones, in no pain, and ready.

• • •

WORD SPREAD QUICKLY that Michelle, Louisville's own "Snow-baby" of 1994, had passed away. News stations called the family home, but Michelle's father, Ed, did not want to speak to anyone. Ashley fielded the calls with poise and grace. Ashley called Bekki Friesen, not wanting Michelle's liver donor family to learn about her passing through the media. The next day, while she was awash in her own grief, Ashley posted a note to Michelle's medical team:

"I want to take a moment to thank all the doctors, surgeons, and nurses that worked so hard trying to save my sister. They were superheroes. They were very nice to us, answered all of our questions, and allowed us all to be in the room with her, even after visiting hours. And when we decided for comfort care they were all so caring. Her kidney doctor came, our transplant nurse coordinator came, and Courtnie, one of our nurses who had taken care of us in the past, came. They all hugged us and cried with us. Everyone at Jewish hospital has been great over the years. From the doctors, to the sur-

geons, and to all the amazing nurses on 3, the old transplant
floor. We have spent a lot of time at Jewish over the years,
and at some points it was our second home. They became
our second family. I cherish the friendships we've made there
over the years."

David, Ashley, Crystal, and Ed made decisions about the funeral,
difficult to do during COVID restrictions. They knew they would
have a crowd of people wanting to attend. In the end, their old
church, Adventure Christian, agreed to host the funeral without
any attendance limitations.

Thursday, May 13, turned out to be a beautiful spring day, cool,
sunny, with a slight breeze and a few clouds passing by as friends
filed in to the church. David wrote his comments out and asked a
relative to read them for him at the service. He said:

*"My love for Michelle has grown so strongly from the day we
both said 'I do' until the day I left her bedside. In those six
years, we had our good and bad days of course, but when
I look back, every day I got to spend with her was a blessing. Being married to Michelle really matured me as a person.
Knowing her story, and all that she went through when she
was younger and the way she always fought and made the
most of every day, made me love her even more. . . I thought
I had years to spend with her. The most painful thing that I
had to do in my life is the one thing I never wanted to do: let
her go. Although we've lost a daughter, a sister, best friend,
and wife, God has a beautiful angel with him now. Take it
from me: Don't take life for granted. Enjoy the time you have
with your loved ones. Because you never know when there
won't be another time to do so. I love you, Michelle, and I'll
miss you forever."*

At Ed's request, Crystal read his letter to his youngest daughter:

"My Dearest Michelle,
This past week has been the most difficult time of my life.

I watched you grow from a very sick little girl into a beautiful, smart, caring, and loving young woman who succeeded in graduating from college, met and married David, and started your career . . .

You accomplished these things when there were times that were hard, medically. You never gave up on anything. You touched a lot of people in your short life and a lot of people touched you!

I am glad you are in heaven with your mom, Grandma, Papaw, Brian, Amy, and a host of others that went before you. Your body is whole again with no pain, no suffering, no meds . . .

Your death has left me heartbroken. I will always be there for David, Chewie, and Reesie. I know how much you loved all three. Honey I am so proud of you and I will miss you desperately until we meet again. To others you were the Snowbaby; to me you were just MY BABY."

Crystal shared wonderful memories of their friendship, filling the room with laughter. She added:

"As a trio, we used to joke that we were going to live well into our nineties and that we would all 'go down together' somehow. We wanted to spend our eighties having walker and wheelchair races in the nursing home where we all three would live. We planned on causing havoc everywhere we went . . . But Ashley and I will carry on, knowing that Michelle is always with us. My twenty-three-year friendship with Michelle did not end this week; she's always with me, my guardian angel, my forever friend."

Finally, Ashley spoke, saying:

I couldn't have imagined my life without her. We were in and out of the hospital a lot over the years. Sometimes together, sometimes on holidays and sometimes on birthdays. We were always there for each other and leaned on each other for sup-

port. *We knew what each other was going through and how they felt.*

Don't get me wrong; we still had plenty of fights, disagreements, and arguments over thirty years, just as any siblings do . . . We were a lot alike in ways but also different in a lot of ways. She was always early and on time. I am always running a few minutes late. I am the better driver and if you don't believe me, ask around! She bit her fingernails, and I didn't. She loved to dress up; I'm good with a hoodie and sweats. We both have a passion and love for animals. Christmas was our favorite holiday, and we both have a love for Jesus. We got baptized at the same time, did Bible study groups together, and went to church together for many years . . .

I never imagined that she would be gone this soon. If I could have saved her by switching places with her, I would have. But then she would be going through this terrible pain and loss instead of me. Right now, she's happy up in heaven. So, if I can take this pain and loss for her, I will.

Little sis, I love you so much. The pain I have felt over this past week has been like no other. A lot of people knew you as the Snowbaby, but I knew you as my little sister, as "Chelle." And I look forward to the day where I can join you in heaven and be reunited.

Ashley closed her thoughts by reciting some of the lyrics from "I Can Only Imagine," with one slight revision:

"I can only imagine, what it will be like, when I walk by yours and Jesus' side, I can only imagine . . ."

• • •

IN AN INTERVIEW with WAVE 3 News just one day after Michelle died, Ashley summed up the family's feelings:

"She was passionate, caring and loving to everyone, she treated everyone equally. We went through a lot with each other growing up and we leaned on each other growing up because we both knew what we were going through . . . she wanted

to help other people because we've had so many people help us."

Ashley's next comments, so gracious for a young woman still reeling from the shock of such searing loss, put the loss in perspective:

"The fact that we made it to our thirties, that we were able to get our driver's license, go to prom, do the things that people kind of take for granted because they know they're going to do them . . . with us, we never even dreamed of reaching sixteen years old . . ."

She went on to mention everyone who had a hand in getting Michelle to Nebraska that fateful day in 1994.

"They allowed us twenty-seven more years with her, so she wouldn't have even been here to make all those memories with us if it wasn't for all of them, so thank you."[9]

In Loving Memory of

Michelle Leigh (Schmitt) Cobble

Entered Into This Life
December 3, 1990

Entered Into Eternal Life
May 7, 2021

Funeral Ceremony
11:00 am Thursday, May 13, 2021
Adventure Christian Church
3321 Ruckriegel Parkway

Officiant
Pastor Phillip Branan

Interment
Resthaven Memorial Park

Program from Michelle Schmitt's funeral, provided by Sharon Stevens Evans.

ASHLEY SCHMITT

Ashley grew and thrived alongside her sister. The two did everything together, even both needing a kidney transplant in 2011, within months of each other. They enjoyed going to movies and concerts together, often with best friend, Crystal Olafson.

Ashley graduated from Seneca High School in Louisville in 2006, went on to earn a BA in Business Administration, then an MBA in Healthcare Management. Like Michelle, Ashley was drawn to a career in healthcare, and as of this writing is in senior management in a national oncological pharmaceutical company.

For a long time after the kidney transplants, both girls had enjoyed relatively good health, though they had to be extremely cautious during the pandemic.

Michelle and Ashley in 2015. Photo used by permission of Glamour Shots Licensing Inc. d/b/a Glamour Shots

For the first week after Michelle's funeral, Ashley struggled deeply. Taking another week off from work, she slept most of the time, or lay still watching the television. She recalls, "I had no interest in doing anything or going anywhere. My dad was starting to worry about me, asking when I was planning on going back to work. I went back the next week, reluctantly. The following week, I became ill."

Ashley had not been eating or drinking well. In June, just a month after Michelle's passing, Ashley was hospitalized, suffering from a stomach virus and dehydration. Considering Michelle's cause of death was a stomach aneurysm, this episode was certainly a stressful time for both Ashley and her father.

Months slowly ticked by, marked by stark reminders that Michelle was no longer with them. For a long time after we lose a loved one, memories pop up of the last holiday, the last conversation, or the first birthday or solo trip after our loss.

Ashley recalled the last Disney movie they enjoyed together, and will never forget that Michelle's last words were to her, on their last phone call just before she lost consciousness. She was struck thinking about her first concert since Michelle passed away. The two had tickets to see a Lauren Daigle concert in 2020, but it was postponed because of COVID. By the time the concert came around again, Michelle had passed away. That November, just six months after losing Michelle, Ashley invited Crystal to use Michelle's ticket, and the two drove to Lexington, Kentucky, for a night full of praise and worship music.

Finally, the year drew to a close. Ashley wrote:

"2021 was anything but easy. Michelle passed away; I was admitted to the hospital for the first time in seven years, ended up having surgeries in both eyes, was in a car wreck, and more. The shots this year just kept coming. Experiencing so many firsts without Michelle was something I never imagined or wanted. This year has tested me in every way possible. It's taught me what true faith is. The pain I've felt this year I never knew existed or had ever experienced before. I've been angry, sad, frustrated, and everything in between.

Everything with Michelle happened so quickly. We've been hospitalized hundreds of times over the years, but we always came home, so I never expected anything less this time around. When she didn't, that was devastating, heartbreaking, and traumatizing. My brain still can't process that she is gone; it doesn't feel real.

I'm sad to see this year go because it's the last one she was alive for. But I also can't wait to see it go as it's been a rough one.

I'm thankful for all of my family and friends that helped me get through this year and for the new friendships I've made."

The next couple of years were full of a long list of firsts and lasts. Ashley bought her first house and enjoyed all of the firsts that go along with that milestone, only without her sister to share it with.

As of this writing, Ashley and her father share her new home together, still in the Louisville area, and she is doing well, excited about the next milestone in her family's incredible story.

ED SCHMITT

After returning home from Omaha, Ed's parents continued to help with the girls while Ed returned to his outdoor work. As the girls grew up, enjoying their lives, working and studying, and giving back through their volunteer work, Ed still found himself struggling with all he had been through with losing his wife, going through the traumas both girls experienced, and with the extreme sacrifices it took to provide and care for his family.

For a long while, he confessed, he was angry with God for all that had happened and had stopped attending church—until the day many years later that Ashley and Michelle made the decision to be baptized. He attended that joyous occasion but was not comfortable being around such a large congregation. In 2010, the girls began attending Adventure Christian Church with their friend Crystal, and one night they were going to share their story together from the pulpit. Ed attended, and felt at home in this little church, enjoying the pastor's sermons as he began to attend Sunday mornings with his daughters. After so many years, he seemed to have found a way to reconnect with his faith.

For the next several years, life took on a naturally quick pace, full of all the experiences you want for your children, with just a few health setbacks along the way. In 2015, Michelle married David Cobble. Life was good, but change was on the way, as it was for all of us. The year 2020 brought new challenges as the girls would need to take extra precautions to protect themselves from COVID. Fourteen months later, in May 2021, as you have read, Michelle suffered a stomach aneurysm and passed away less than forty-eight hours later, a devastating loss. She was buried on May 13, Ed's birthday.

In the two years since Michelle's passing, the movie and book surrounding their experience came out. In many ways, this public exposure forced Ed into many uncomfortable situations once again, where he would need to face crowds of people he had never met, speak with the media, talk about his family's experience, and relive memories that were both painful and overwhelming, full of many mountaintop moments, terrifying valleys, and unimaginable loss.

Sharon Stevens Evans and Ed Schmitt reunite at a private viewing of the movie,
"Ordinary Angels." Photo courtesy: Leslie Turner.

Though it has been an emotional and extremely difficult time adjusting to Michelle's passing, the renewed attention has helped him realize that his daughters' stories are inspiring many people once again. After a long period of being away from church fellowship, Ed now attends a new church with Ashley. He has never remarried. Ed continues to work hard in the lawn care business.

SHARON STEVENS

Sharon's time fulfilling her calling to help the Schmitt family was an extraordinary period, just one part of her incredible life, with more drama, highs, and lows to come.

After Michelle's surgery, Sharon returned to the salon, continuing to work with Angels, Inc. for only a short time. For many years she remained close to Ashley and Michelle, but eventually their connection dissipated, until a long time would go by without any contact between Sharon and anyone in the Schmitt family. In 2007, Sharon would finally marry a man whom she described as her soulmate, Perry Evans.

In 2010, Sharon suffered a serious head injury after a truck crossed the median and struck her car at a high rate of speed, an injury that affects her to this day. Three years later, Perry passed away suddenly from a head injury suffered during heavy rains that hit the Louisville area on April 3, 2015. Sharon explains, "He gave me the love and confidence to forge ahead, just like the girls did, and claim a happy, loving life beyond the gloom in my past. He uplifted my spirit with simple laughter and acceptance."

In the years that followed, Sharon struggled to find her footing. Single, in her seventies, and struggling with sometimes debilitating residual effects from her head injury along with the natural effects of aging, Sharon would note some similarities in what may be the last twenty years of her life to her first twenty years. People have taken advantage of her, abused her, conned and deserted her, undervalued and definitely underestimated her. Like many in our seventies-plus population, she remains vulnerable and too trusting but fiercely independent.

Along the way, ordinary angels continue to show up in marvelous ways. Her oldest son, Derek, keeps her grounded when symptoms of her brain injury rise to the surface and keeps close tabs on her. And in 2019, another unexpected angel contacted Sharon.

In the first year after the blizzard and Michelle's triumphant return to Louisville, Sharon had a lot to process. Looking back, how was she able to push forward through seemingly insurmountable odds in her own life to play her part in the many miracles woven throughout this story? At Derek's urging, Sharon began writing everything down to the finest detail, just as it happened, then kept writing, going back through her own survival story.

The threads of God's grace and protection, of people placed throughout her life who would become her own ordinary angels, and how everything would weave together to prepare her for the events that led up to January 17, 1994, were easy to see. So were her own flaws and failures, sutures and scars. This was not a boastful résumé of accomplishment

Sharon Stevens Evans, July 2023.
Photo credit: Bruce Morris, Morris Images

but a story that would show the reader that we are all capable of making a difference, of receiving God's grace and being used by him, regardless of our past, or how the world may measure us.

• • •

AN AGENT SHOPPED the story to studios, actors, and others who were interested in bringing it to the big screen, and for many years, the story was optioned, released, and then optioned again. To be "optioned" means someone buys the temporary rights to a story, then has a limited time to start production. At the end of that period, they can renew or release their rights for someone else to pick up. Twenty-five difficult years went by as the story sat, undeveloped. Then, unexpectedly, everything changed.

THE EXTRAORDINARY ORIGIN OF THE MOVIE

In 2019, Lionsgate studio partnered with Kingdom Story Company, and Vertigo/Stampede Productions to produce a film based on Sharon's story, which would ultimately be titled *Ordinary Angels*. Then, in 2020, the COVID pandemic put a halt to the project. Sharon's story seemed as if it would never be produced, but as health restrictions lifted, production began, and Sharon turned her focus to getting this book published in time for the release of the movie. It would take another string of miracles for everything to come together, but in a very real way, the movie and book projects have given Sharon a fresh wind.

Both projects she hopes will be a legacy that might help other people to see God's hand in their lives, to say yes when God gives them a challenge, or perhaps to find the strength and will to move forward out of an abusive or alcoholic situation, or find help and healing for present or past issues with mental illness or painful memories. Maybe someone will decide to become an organ donor because of this story and save someone else's life. Sharon may very well have another defining moment ahead of her, another opportunity to say yes, but in the meantime, this story, in both book and movie, can carry on her calling long after she is unable to do so.

• • •

In October 2022, Sharon, Ashley and Ed Schmitt, Crystal Olafson, and others were invited by director Jon Gunn to a private first cut viewing of *Ordinary Angels* at Showcase Cinemas in Louisville, Kentucky. With only family and close friends invited, the evening was a wonderful opportunity for Sharon, Derek, Ashley, Ed, and others to reunite, and to see themselves portrayed on the big screen by an incredible cast of esteemed actors. Two of the film's producers, Tony Young and Kevin Downes, came in town for the viewing and met, for the first time, these individuals whose lives, forever altered by those events, they immortalized on film.

After a time of introductions and mingling in the lobby, everyone took their seats in the theater, these select few feeling nervous and excited about what they were about to see. Watching such a pivotal time in your life condensed into a movie with all of the creative alterations that must inevitably take place requires both courage and grace. As the lights in the theater dimmed to black, a cheer rose up. Throughout the movie, one could hear both laughter and tears, gasps and cheers from across the room, and at the end of the movie the audience rose up with fervent applause, knowing absolutely this movie would be amazing: full of intense struggle, heartwarming moments, dramatic obstacles, and thrilling triumph, perfectly acted and directed, with stunning special effects.

At a private viewing of *Ordinary Angels* in Louisville, Kentucky, from left to right: Tony Young (Kingdom Story Company), Ashley Schmitt, director Jon Gunn, Sharon Stevens, Ed Schmitt, and Kevin Downes (Kingdom Story Company). Photo courtesy: Paul Turner

Afterward, guests trickled out as the people who had worked so hard and risked so much in producing and directing the movie lingered for a while to enjoy a chance to celebrate with Sharon, Ashley, Ed, and others close to the story.

• • •

BY THE TIME this book was ready to go to print, previews for the major motion picture *Ordinary Angels* were already showing in theaters nationwide. The movie, starring two-time Oscar-winning actress Hilary Swank as Sharon Stevens (*Million Dollar Baby, Boys Don't Cry, Freedom Writers, Alaska Daily*), Alan Ritchson as Ed Schmitt (*Reacher, Hunger Games: Catching Fire, Teenage*

Mutant Ninja Turtles), Nancy Travis as Barbara Schmitt (*The Kominsky Method, Last Man Standing, Three Men and a Baby*), among others and was directed by Jon Gunn (*The Case for Christ, Like Dandelion Dust, Unbreakable Boy*) based on a screenplay by Meg Tilly and Kelly Fremon Craig.

It follows on the heels of Kingdom Story Company's tremendous slate of highly successful uplifting films, beginning with *I Can Only Imagine* (2018), *I Still Believe* (2020), *Jesus Music* (2021), *American Underdog* (2021), *Johnny Cash: The Redemption of an American Icon* (2022), and *Jesus Revolution* (2023).

The path to producing any movie is arduous, but bringing *Ordinary Angels* to the screen was a journey full of twists and turns, miraculous interventions, and unexpected players, a story that will be told by the pioneering and visionary leaders of Kingdom Story Company, Jon Erwin, Andrew Erwin, Kevin Downes, and Tony Young.

At a private viewing of *Ordinary Angels* in Louisville, Kentucky, from left to right: Sharon Stevens, director Jon Gunn, and Sharon's son Derek Young. Photo courtesy: Paul Turner.

Without spoiling any of the movie's plot, this is a good time to acknowledge that the studio took some dramatic license with the script to shorten the story but still get Sharon's obstacles across. The writers did so with Sharon's full knowledge and blessing. For example, from the book, you would know that Sharon was not an alcoholic, though her life growing up in a home deeply affected by alcoholism left her with many of the same scars. We do not want to diminish the reality of alcoholism and other addictions and illnesses in many lives, nor the effects it can have on a family. Resources in the next few pages provide help for both those struggling with addiction of any kind and for their loved ones, who often learn unhealthy behaviors from their situation and pass them on to the next generation.

From the book, you would know that Sharon's relationship with her son Derek was never strained. Derek is a great source of love and strength for Sharon, and always has been. Sharon did have a difficult relationship within her family for many years.

At this time in her life, Sharon enjoys time with both of her sons, now grown. As with all of us, relationships with our loved ones go through seasons and can be challenging as we age, but today, Sharon feels blessed and loved.

DAVE STONE ON BEING AN ORDINARY ANGEL

Just a few months before the movie premiere, Sharon had the joy of meeting for the first time now-retired Southeast Christian pastor Dave Stone and his wife, Beth. Dave not only had a heaven-sent role in getting Michelle to the airport on time, but was also portrayed in the movie. His insights about that dramatic moment in the story were inspiring:

From left to right: Sharon Stevens Evans, Pastor Dave Stone, and wife Beth Stone. Photo courtesy: Dave Stone

Over one hundred people had dropped what they were doing that frigid winter day and quickly responded to help. Soon the helicopter ascended and was gone. It felt like we were all participating in a relay race. We had run our leg of the race, and now we had handed the baton on to the helicopter pilot to use his giftings and talents. At the time I did not know Sharon Stevens, but it's obvious that two years before, she was the first runner in this relay—and she ran it well.

I appreciated all of those who came to help out that day. Serving others has a way of uniting people. Service is the great equalizer and it also can make you look more like Jesus. Maybe that's why he said in Mark 10:45 that he did not come to be served but to serve.

Other than me, everyone else who was there that day had heard about an immediate need and willingly chose to come and do their part. But even though my presence that day was accidental, my daughter and I felt so good inside. In fact we couldn't wait to get

back home to share what we experienced. Savannah burst through
our front door and exclaimed, "Mommy, Mommy we got to help
someone!"

It's truly incredible when a community comes together to accom-
plish something, completely unconcerned about who gets the credit.
Earlier I said that my presence was accidental, but I know better
than that. The timing was too perfect. Providential would be a
more fitting word. After that experience it made me want to serve
more. God will intersect your lives with people who are in need.
Then it just comes down to whether you are willing to follow that
prompting and get involved, like Sharon did.

Sometimes we think, "Well what could little old me do? I don't
have much to offer. My giftings aren't in securing private jets or
raising tens of thousands of dollars."

But may I point out that in that snowy church parking lot,
not one of those people was a professional snow remover. They
just made themselves available and did what was needed in that
moment. Just because you can't do everything doesn't mean you
can't do something.

I'm not asking you to be a "Sharon." I'm just asking you to
grab a shovel, and head to wherever you are needed the most. Be
an "ordinary angel" for someone else. And when you serve it will
awaken something inside of you because you've taken the focus off
of yourself and placed it on others. I guarantee that if you do, in
your heart, the child within you will cry out with excitement, "I
got to help somebody! I got to help somebody!"

Dave Stone pastored at Southeast Christian Church for another
twenty-five years. He and his wife Beth still live in the Louisville
area. His daughter Savannah now resides in Evansville, Indiana.
The day they got to help the "snow baby" is one of her earliest and
best memories.

The church continues to be known for serving in the community
in a variety of ways. Several years later Southeast outgrew those
facilities on Hikes Lane and moved eight miles away where they
built a new campus. But the Hikes Lane church will always hold a
special place in their hearts—not just because of what took place
in the sanctuary, but also for what happened in the parking lot that
one divine day in 1994.

Resources

Do you or a loved one struggle with alcohol or other addictions, mental illness, sexual abuse, or domestic violence? Find help here.

SUBSTANCE ABUSE

Sharon is depicted as an alcoholic in the movie, a dramatic license the studio took to shorten the story but still get her obstacles across. In real life, Sharon turned away from alcohol because of her family history, but suffered from many of the same tendencies, as the child of two alcoholics. If you saw yourself on either side of her childhood stories, even if your experience was years in the past, it is not too late to get help. You will find many resources, groups, and other support right in your own community, or you can tap into online groups and resources from the privacy of your own home. If you or a loved one is currently in danger, call 911. Otherwise, you may want to start here:

- Alcoholics Anonymous: https://www.aa.org
- Al-Anon/Alateen: https://al-anon.org/
- Narcotics Anonymous: https://na.org/

MENTAL/EMOTIONAL ILLNESS, SELF-HARM

Sometimes substance abuse or self-harm is our way of coping with extreme emotional distress, mental illness, or other trauma, as may have been the case with Sharon's mother. If you or a family member struggle with extreme changes in mental or emotional stability, or have tried or considered self-harm or suicide, find help below. If you or a loved one is in a crisis right now, call 911. Otherwise, you may want to start here:

- Suicide and Mental Health Crisis hotline: 988
- National Alliance on Mental Illness: https://www.nami.org

SEXUAL ABUSE/SURVIVORS OF SEXUAL ABUSE

Sharon is a survivor of sexual abuse, not just as a child, but also as an adult, a story not shared in this book. If you or a loved one is struggling as either a recent victim or someone who experienced sexual abuse in years past, find anonymous, confidential help here.

If you or a loved one is in imminent danger right now, get to a safe place and call 911. Otherwise, you may want to start here:

- Rape, Abuse, and Incest National Network: https://www.rainn.org/ or call (800)656-4673 (HOPE).
- Adult Survivors of Child Abuse: https://www.ascasupport.org/

DOMESTIC VIOLENCE

Sharon experienced domestic violence at the hands of her mother and, later, at the hands of a spouse, a story not included in this book. You may be in immediate danger right now, along with those under your care. If so, get to a safe place and call 911. Otherwise, you may want to start here for anonymous, confidential help:

- National Domestic Violence Hotline: 800-799-7233 (SAFE)
- National Coalition Against Domestic Violence: https://ncadv.org/get-help

In all of these cases, you are not alone.

ORGAN DONATION/LIVER SUPPORT

Michelle, Ashley, and Crystal all volunteered their time to raise awareness about organ donation, an act of kindness needed across all races and cultures to ensure everyone on the waiting list has a chance to find a match. The simplest way to confirm your interest in being an organ, eye, or tissue donor in the event of your death is to say yes to the organ donation question when you renew your driver's license. You can also register or learn more information about donor programs at:

- https://www.registerme.org
- https://www.donatelife.net/
- https://www.americantransplantfoundation.org/
- https://www.organdonor.gov

There are also many sites focused on providing funding, support, and education for families needing an organ match. Ask your health care provider for more information.

You can donate a kidney, part of your liver, skin, and, of course, blood and plasma as a living donor. Both of the first two organizations above give you the option of registering as a living donor. If you have a family member or loved one in need, you can also direct your donation to that person.

- Kidney donation: https://www.kidneyregistry.org/
- Blood and plasma donation: https://www.redcrossblood.org/
- Support and resources for those living with a progressive hereditary liver disease can be found through the PFIC Advocacy and Resource Network, Inc. (Progressive Familial Intrahepatic Cholestasis) at PFIC.org.

CONTACT THE AUTHOR OR PUBLISHER

Were you touched by the author's story, or do you have questions about this book? Would you like to be notified when the audiobook is released? Subscribe at encouragepublishing.com or send us a message including "Ordinary Angels" in the subject line to: info@encouragebooks.com.

You may also reach Sharon or inquire about bulk sales or appearances through her publisher:
ENCOURAGE PUBLISHING
INFO@ENCOURAGEBOOKS.COM
WWW.ENCOURAGEPUBLISHING.COM

Team Credits

Ordinary Angels is the product of a team of dedicated professionals and volunteer contributors for whom we are extremely grateful and wish to give credit:

- Author: Sharon Stevens Evans
- Prologue and Epilogue: Leslie Turner, with contributions by David Cobble, Kevin Downes (Kingdom Story Company), Orin and Bekki Friesen, Crystal Olafson, Ashley Schmitt, Ed Schmitt, and Dave Stone
- Developmental editor: Leslie Turner
- Copy editor: Kirsten Herman
- Proofing: Lisa Grimenstein
- Original edit: John Nelson
- Cover and interior design: Jonathan Lewis
- Back cover and author photography: Bruce Morris
- Story consultation: Derek Young

Encourage Publishing has multiple imprints, including *Encourage Books, Encourage Music, Encourage Kids, Wildfly, Turner Creative,* and *Alienta!* Learn more about Encourage Publishing, our titles, and our submission requirements at encouragepublishing.com.

ENCOURAGE
PUBLISHING
NEW ALBANY, INDIANA
WWW.ENCOURAGEPUBLISHING.COM

Endnotes

[1]Jim Adams, "Louisville Family Is Bearing Up under Crushing Burden of Crises," *Louisville Courier-Journal*, Thursday, August 13, 1992, B2. Image © The Courier-Journal – USA TODAY NETWORK, licensed through USAToday/Imagn.

[2]Gardiner Harris, "Michelle, 3, Comes Home with New Liver and New Life," *Louisville Courier-Journal*, March 13, 1994, B1.

[3]Jim Adams, "Louisville Family Is Bearing Up under Crushing Burden of Crises," *Louisville Courier-Journal*, Thursday, August 13, 1992, B2.

[4]IAdams, "Louisville Family Is Bearing Up."

[5]Adams, "Louisville Family is Bearing Up.".

[6]140 Cong. Rec. 11 (Tuesday, February 8, 1994).

[7]UPMC Pediatrics, "Rare Diseases: What Is Byler Disease?" December 6, 2022, https://share.upmc.com/2022/12/what-is-byler-disease/?source=archive_title.

[8]Matthew Glowicki, "The Blizzard of 1994 . . . Paralyzed Louisville, Gave Rise to Heroism," *Louisville Courier-Journal*, January 17, 2019, A1.

[9]Stephen Goin, "'People All Over Came to Help': Louisville 'Snow Baby,' Michelle Schmitt, Dies at 30," May 8, 2021, [Video] *Wave3.com*, https://www.wave3.com/2021/05/08/people-all-over-came-help-louisville-snow-baby-michelle-schmitt-dies/.